The Saab-Scania Story

Foreword

With the attainment of Saab's 50th anniversary in 1987 and Scania's centenary in 1991, Saab-Scania will have completed 150 years of progress within five years — a notable achievement and one well worthy of celebration! For to have been an aircraft builder for 50 years and an automaker for almost a century places the Company in the ranks of the pioneers.

Our first products included kerosene-burning automobiles with horizontal cylinders and propeller aircraft powered by piston engines — items symbolic of the very infancy of motoring and aviation. Much has happened since then. We have adopted new technologies, witnessed the many phases of technical progress and authored many significant innovations. In short, we have been intimately involved in shaping the course of developments.

The reflection of these developments in our products down through the years has prompted the publication of this volume, which tells the story of the entire range of aircraft from the Saab 17 to the JAS 39 Gripen, and cars from the pristine 92 to the Saab 9000.

Saab-Scania products are the tangible results of decades of accumulated knowledge and experience gathered from both our successes and failures — a 'reservoir' of knowhow passed from generation to generation, and from product to product. In this context, what could be more appropriate than to describe the results of our labors? Or to dedicate this book to all our employees, past and present — those who contributed to making Saab-Scania what it is today and their successors who continue to work for its prosperity?

Since it is the Saab in Saab-Scania which celebrates its jubilee on this occasion, the book will deal mainly with aircraft and cars. (The turn of Scania's trucks and buses will come in 1991.) However, since the story from 1969 on is also that of Saab-Scania (Saab and Scania-Vabis having merged that year), it is appropriate that it should include a portrayal of Scania, both in a historical perspective and as it exists today.

The Company has undergone a process of continuous development and change according as its cars and aircraft have evolved. In common with all

industrial concerns, it has been obliged to adapt continuously to changing conditions, both within the organization and in the world about it.

Saab – or Svenska Aeroplan Aktiebolaget – was founded in 1937 as the cornerstone of an effective Swedish aircraft industry, at a time when the clouds of war were beginning to gather over Europe. In 1945, in the hope of a lasting peace, the Company decided to scale down its production of military aircraft and to develop its civilian operations – a change in policy signified by the appearance of the Saab 90 Scandia airliner and the Saab 92 car.

The advent of the Cold War, followed by the outbreak of the Korean War – events which demanded that all available capacity be devoted to the production of military aircraft – resulted in the demise of the Scandia. Fortunately, however, car production had arrived to stay.

The 50s, 60s and 70s were characterized by continuity and expansion. During this period, Saab developed and built military aircraft, mainly for the Swedish Defense Forces, and small cars for the Scandinavian market.

By the end of the 1970s, the Company had arrived at something of a crossroads. It was again clear that our survival as an independent and expanding aircraft manufacturer would require not only greater concentration on the civilian market, but expansion on an international scale. A future based on the production of matériel for the Swedish Air Force – regardless of the significance of this activity to Saab-Scania or the nation – would no longer be viable. Furthermore, it had become apparent that our continued existence as an automaker would depend on the development of more exclusive models, mainly for export.

This was the background to a series of major decisions taken by the Board in the late 70s and early 80s, regarding the future 'mix' of automotive and aerospace products. From these emerged the Saab 9000, the RBS15 anti-shipping missile, the Saab SF340 airliner, the JAS 39 Gripen military aircraft, the Viking research satellite and the Tele-X communications satellite.

The Saab SF340 differs from the other products in that it represents Saab-Scania's commitment to a completely new area – that of civil aviation. Since the

essentially long-term nature of all industrial projects applies particularly to the automotive and aviation industries, the successful development of this activity will demand precisely the same qualities of perseverance and patience as those applied to the car and truck sectors at the development stage. Saab-Scania has inherited these qualities.

The renewal of our product range was accompanied by greater selectivity in our areas of operation, concentration being laid on the automotive and aerospace sectors, with particular emphasis on specific market segments. A more market-oriented organizational structure was also introduced.

These developments are described in the chronicle of events and in the various articles dealing with individual topics. The latter describe the transformation of Saab-Scania from a small manufacturer producing mainly for Scandinavia into a major industrial group developing and making products for world markets.

The decisions taken in 1979–80 were characterized by the high level of risk involved and by the projected time scale of the effects. This, combined with the fact that Saab-Scania's financial position at the time was by no means compara-ble with its standing today, made the decisions significant not only in them-selves, but as testimony to the Company's faith in the future. These commit-ments were made on the basis of one factor alone — our people.

The outstanding professionalism and involvement of our personnel form the very foundation on which our hopes for the future are based, justifying the substantial investments which we have made in the past and will continue to make in the future. Given the necessary skills, we may indeed go forward with confidence.

These attributes are complemented by an extremely healthy balance sheet, a factor which will enable us to continue with our massive investment in research and development projects, in new product ranges and in new production tech-nologies — all funded by our own resources. The ability of a company to finance its own future investment programs is always a major strength — particularly when substantial risks are involved.

In short, our current situation may be regarded as an ideal platform on which to build for the future. Apart from our traditions and the quality of our work-force, we possess a number of other advantages which make us unique — assets which we shall continue to guard and exploit.

One of these is our involvement in the development of state-of-the-art tech-nologies, particularly for application to our range of military products. This is of major importance to engineering standards generally, not only within Saab-Scania but throughout the nation as a whole.

The benefits of including aerospace and automotive operations in the same group are illustrated by many examples, above all by the spin-off activities derived from the military sector — cars, airliners, missiles and space vehicles — and the various other high-tech activities of the Combitech Group (which might be described as Saab-Scania's entrepreneur in the area of leading-edge tech-nologies).

Although these activities have long since become fully-fledged operations in their own right, abundant opportunities for technical cooperation and technology transfer between individual companies still exist. While we have come a long way, much remains to be done. The potential is enormous.

Despite the strength of our current situation, we are only too well aware of how fast-moving and tough international competition can be. Our situation represents nothing more than a satisfactory 'starting point', and the road ahead will be difficult!

In the field of aerospace, our objective will be to play a leading role in building the commuter airliners of the future, while our military aircraft and missiles (together with successive refinements of these systems) will continue to contribute to the strengthening of Sweden's air defenses. This requires that we be vigilant in safeguarding the aircraft and missile industry which we have built up with such perseverance.

Car manufacturing operations have undergone rapid expansion during the 80s — a trend which is expected to continue in the foreseeable future. The growth in output and international success which we have achieved have created the conditions for consolidating this activity, and we must now work to secure our position in the long term.

Scania Division is faced with the task of penetrating the last major truck market remaining to it — the USA. This will be approached in typical Scania fashion — quietly, calmly and purposefully — with the aim of establishing the same type of secure foothold enjoyed by our trucks in other markets.

Living up to these aspirations will demand will-power and resources, as well as expertise. For this reason, the Company has initiated a program of renewal entitled 'One step ahead', the first phase of which will be launched as part of Saab's 50th anniversary celebrations and which will conclude with Scania's centenary — a process which will involve all employees at home and abroad, harnessing the spirit of enterprise which resides within us all.

And, as in all commercial enterprises, a modicum of luck will be needed to go with the other prerequisites!

It is a truism that one and one do not always make two. (In the case of Saab and Scania, the total — as we have already seen — was 150.) As proof that the main purpose of the merger — optimum utilization of the companies' combined resources — has been achieved, Saab-Scania today occupies a position in the forefront of specialized transport technology.

In a sense, the wheel has come full circle. In 1984, when the Company introduced its new logo, the design was intended to represent its combined historical associations. In this context, no symbol seemed more appropriate than the griffin — the mythical creature which is proudly displayed on the arms of the province of Skåne and which appeared on the hood of the first Scania automobile at the turn of the century (Scania, of course, being the Latin for Skåne). The chain was completed with the Company's decision to expand its production of Saab cars (on which the griffin has been restored to its position of eminence) by building a new plant in Malmö, capital of Skåne, where Saab-Scania has its roots.

The coincidence whereby the JAS aircraft unveiled on Saab's 50th anniversary was christened the Gripen (or Griffin) now appears to have been preordained.

It is our earnest hope that the qualities of tradition and renewal symbolized by our logo will continue to characterize the Saab-Scania of the future.

Sten Gustafsson
Chairman of the Board

Georg Karnsund
President and Chief Executive Officer

Prologue

Enoch Leonard Thulin — the aeronautical engineer who took his doctorate in 1912, the airman who made the first return crossing of the Baltic Sea in 1913 and the entrepreneur who founded Sweden's first aircraft industry in 1914.

In 1936 — the year in which the Air Force acquired the Sk12 — the Government allocated 80 million kronor to the Army, 39 million to the Navy and 28 million to the Air Force.

It all started with Enoch Thulin — the pioneer who, in 1914, established Sweden's first full-scale aircraft factory at Landskrona, employing over 1,000 people by 1918. Sadly, Thulin was to die when one of his own creations crashed in 1919 and the enterprise collapsed with the liquidation of his company the following year. Although several interested parties attempted to take over the operation, the Air Board (which was responsible for matériel procurement on behalf of the defense services at the time) considered none of them capable of competing with the new aircraft which were available from abroad.

At the time, this was the end of aircraft production by private industry in Sweden. The Army Air Corps was supplying about 70% of its own requirements and the Navy Air Service was importing most of its planes. Furthermore, being peacetime, the air defense budget was small and it was impossible to predict whether future parliaments would allocate more finance. As a result, the aviation market was uncertain and major investors were loath to invest capital.

Svenska Aero AB was established in 1921. The principals behind the new company were German aircraft manufacturers who, under the terms of the Treaty of Versailles, were forbidden to produce airplanes at home. Although the Naval Air Service ordered a number of Heinkels from the company, the affair was shrouded in mystery; the company was never registered and no records detailing its operations have ever been found. Although Heinkel was presumably the major shareholder, Svenska Aero eventually ran into financial difficulties and was acquired by AB Svenska Järnvägsverkstäderna (ASJ) in 1932 — a time when Heinkel's management and design personnel were needed more urgently by the German armaments industry.

Alarmed at the prospect of foreign interests becoming established in Sweden, representatives of Götaverken, Bofors, ASJ, Stora Kopparberg and SKF had already written to the Minister of Defense in 1925, declaring their immediate readiness to establish a Swedish aircraft industry, a communication prompted by the formation of AB Flygindustri in Malmö by parties fronting for the German Junkers company. No response was received from the Government and the company, in any case, collapsed in 1935 despite a promising start.

However, the tramp of jackboots throughout Europe in the mid-30s led to second thoughts and, in 1936, the Government decided to promote the establishment of a domestic defense industry. Announcing the decision, Prime Minister Per Albin Hansson stated: "As far as possible, our nation should produce its own weapons. Every instance in which we have to purchase equipment from abroad makes us more or less dependent on other countries. We have first-class shipyards capable of building warships, and excellent weapon foundries in Eskilstuna and Bofors to equip our army. What we lack are the resources to produce warplanes".

In December 1936, the Prime Minister summoned a meeting of representatives of the Royal Swedish Air Force (RSAF), Bofors, Götaverken and ASJ, to whom he outlined the Government's thinking, adding that, although the work could be shared by a number of small companies, the limited funding available would support only a single industry, and all development activities would have to be coordinated under common management. Although the first aircraft were to be built under license, domestic designs would eventually be introduced.

In view of the substantial investment involved, the newly formed group was to be guaranteed all aircraft orders until 1943.

ASJ and Bofors were clearly interested, while Götaverken offered to produce twelve

planes per year commencing immediately. Prompted by the Government, which was anxious to get the project under way, Bofors submitted articles of incorporation to the Älvsborg County Administration on 2 April 1937, announcing the formation of a new company, Svenska Aeroplan AB, with registered offices at Trollhättan.

The share capital was SKr 4 million ($1.3 million), 1.5 million of which was subscribed by Bofors-Nohab and 2.5 million by AB Ars (part of the Electrolux Group, and like Bofors, one of Axel Wenner-Gren's interests).

With their armaments factory in Bofors and their AB Flygmotor subsidiary, Bofors and Nohab together possessed all the facilities needed to become a Swedish armaments monopoly. Axel Wenner-Gren, Head of Electrolux, was elected Chairman of the Board.

As one of the original parties involved in the discussions, the Government also requested ASJ, which had an aircraft division known as ASJA, to expand its facilities to accommodate future orders.

It was natural that the authorities should propose that the newly established Svenska Aeroplan AB and the reorganized ASJA should cooperate. However, to tell the truth, it must be said that the suggestion created fireworks in certain quarters. Backed by Stockholms Enskilda Bank and Marcus Wallenberg, ASJ demanded equality, whereas Bofors was essentially seeking to dominate the entire matériel supply industry.

The only point of agreement was that

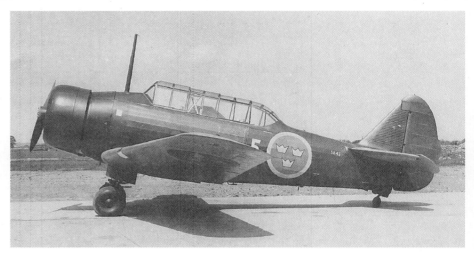

Götaverken could withdraw from the scene. According to the production schedule submitted by the company, it was not itself in a position to fill all the domestic orders for aircraft. Since both the Matériel Administration and the Government required all air defense equipment to be supplied by a single company, they turned to the Bofors Group and ASJ.

The situation was resolved in 1937 by the establishment of a joint company − AB Förenade Flygverkstäder − to apportion future orders between the two member companies.

Since ASJA was already building the B4A, Sk12 and Sk14 under license, pressure on space necessitated the construction of a new aircraft plant at Linköping in 1937. In the same year, Saab began construction of its aircraft factory at Trollhättan.

The NA-16-4M was built under license as the Sk14. The aircraft was operated by the RSAF from 1939 to 1949.

At the outbreak of Second World War in 1939, the Swedish Air Force consisted of about 120 aircraft, organized in 10 to 12 understrength divisions. Equipment included the B4 Hawker Hart, a light bomber.

1937 – THE BEGINNING

The cattle grazed for the last time in the meadows around Tunhem, north of Trollhättan, in the fall of 1937. Poles were stuck in the ground and cords stretched hither and thither, forming incomprehensible patterns — at least to the cows. The new Svenska Aeroplan Aktiebolaget factory was being marked out.

The site had been chosen with care. Between Stallbacka and Hunneberg lay (in the words of a contemporary report) "an area of 1,200 meters in diameter, requiring only to be drained in order to serve as an airfield. Free access from the air is available from two directions. On the left-hand side of the field is the Göta Älv river, 400 meters wide and ideal for use as a flying boat terminal".

And so, the wild duck were also destined, within a few years, to have their peace shattered by the arrival of fantastic birds with equally fantastic names like S17B.

Established with a share capital of SKr 4 million ($1.3 million), the new Com-

Svenska Aeroplan Aktiebolaget's first factory under construction at Tunhemsängarna in Trollhättan.

pany was intended to complement the activities of the Aircraft Division of Svenska Järnvägsverkstäderna (ASJA) at Linköping.

However worn the cliché, the clouds of war were, in fact, gathering over Europe and the Royal Swedish Air Force was in urgent need of re-equipment. Although the existence of two competitors naturally created an ideal situation for the Government as a purchaser, administrative complications and the jealous protection of individual preserves prompted the authorities to request (it might even be said, order) the two parties to form a joint company, AB Förenade Flygverkstäder (AFF), to undertake design and sales. From its headquarters in Stockholm, the company — under the neutral chairmanship of former Cabinet Minister Torsten Nothin — was to direct and develop activities, allocating work impartially to the individual factories.

Svenska Aeroplan Aktiebolaget's first logo.

Saab-Scania and Swedish defense policy

Saab's activities were directly related to Swedish defense policy from the very outset. In 1936, as the threat of war loomed, Parliament decided to establish a Swedish Air Force consisting of five wings equipped with a total of 257 warplanes. The aircraft were to be acquired from foreign as well as Swedish makers. In 1940, after several years of competition with a number of other companies, Saab was given a monopoly to manufacture aircraft under the terms of a framework agreement concluded between it and the Government — a development which was obviously hastened by the recent outbreak of war. (The equipment of the Swedish Air Force was not proceeding as quickly as dictated by the gravity of the situation and time did not permit the luxury of dealing with a number of suppliers.) Neither was there any prospect of purchasing aircraft abroad; all other potential suppliers needed their own aircraft only too well.

Under the terms of the agreement, Saab undertook to develop and manufacture airplanes in accordance with an agreed schedule and to expand its resources as required to fulfill its obligations. The Royal Swedish Air Force Matériel Administration was to place the appropriate orders under the terms of the same plan. Although this was nothing less than a monopoly situation (despite all circumlocution to the contrary), the agreement included detailed provisions governing pricing, control and profits in order to eliminate undesirable effects — an approach which quickly silenced all criticism.

At the end of the War in 1945, the Government appointed a Defense Commission which, in its final report issued in 1947, laid down five principles which were to govern defense matériel procurement policy — production at home, adequate production capacity, supply of the most up-to-date equipment, standardization and efficiency of production.

In 1948, Russian troops blockaded the access routes to the occupied city of Berlin, posing the threat of a third world war only three years after peace had been concluded. To Saab, this meant that all civil aircraft activities had to be abandoned in favor of military requirements. The situation was so serious — and General Bengt Nordenskiöld, (then Commander-in-Chief of the Swedish Air Force) so single-minded — that Parliament approved a Government proposal to im-plement a rolling 7-year equipment delivery program to meet the needs of the Force. Neither the Army nor the Navy had ever been accorded such treatment. Under Nordenskiöld's leadership, the Royal Swedish Air Force became the fourth largest in the world, with 1,007 combat aircraft.

The crisis created by the outbreak of the Korean War in 1950 resulted in the renewal of the contract by mutual agreement. However, it is no exaggeration to say that the matériel procurement policy of the Air Force has not been influenced by external events since then, the subsequent level of military preparedness being adjudged sufficiently high by the Government to obviate the need for any extraordinary defense policy measures directly affecting the Air Force. Nonetheless, the Swedish defense chiefs claimed that national preparedness was not satisfactory, maintaining in a top-secret report that the Air Force should have a much greater number of aircraft at its disposal.

Although a new framework agreement between Saab and the Matériel Administration was signed in 1961, this was not related to the political crisis which shook Europe when the Russians commenced to build the Berlin Wall in August; the original agreement had simply expired. Saab's position in the context of national defense policy was determined solely by Parliamentary decisions to commit economic resources to individual projects. An example was the Viggen project which was undertaken in 1961 and was of such scale as to require a specific development framework. Since avionics (which were not produced by the Company) were beginning to account for an increasing proportion of aircraft costs, Saab's influence on the management and decision-making functions was reduced. In terms of both national security and employment, the importance of the production resources developed by the Company for the Draken project was such that their retention was considered to be vital — a factor which obviously contributed to the decision to proceed with the Viggen.

The defense matériel commission appointed in 1965 was authorized to report on the practicability of abandoning the Viggen. In the event, the proposal was considered impracticable — especially in view of the outstanding technical success of the project.

Although some parliamentary disagree-

ment on defense matters in general and air matériel problems in particular, emerged in the wake of the changes in government which took place in the 70s and 80s, this was attributable more to divergences in economic priorities than to differences in defense policy as such. Differences regardless, the decision to undertake the JAS project was taken in a genuine spirit of democracy and the aircraft is now under development. Although the project may formally be discontinued at any time, the fact that the JAS is currently at the same stage of development as the Viggen

in 1965 would make it equally difficult, in political terms, to abandon the undertaking now. Long-term planning is crucial to the credibility of Swedish defense policy – a credibility founded on the concept of a nation 'armed in peace and neutral in war'.

Saab-Scania will obviously continue to be dependent, to a degree, on the course of Swedish defense policy, although to a lesser extent than in its early days in 1937. The Company's conscious efforts to develop its production of civil aircraft has created, and will continue to create, new markets.

Four generations of combat aircraft, the Lansen, Draken, Viggen and 105 – vigilant defenders of Swedish neutrality for more than 30 years.

11

Arming for peace

Saab-Scania supplies the Swedish Air Force not only with aircraft, but also with vital armament systems and other equipment used by the Army and Navy. The picture shows a Viggen aircraft on a reconnaissance mission with a Spica-class vessel in the background. These ships are armed with RBS15 surface-to-surface missiles supplied by Saab Missiles.

How best may the cooperation developed over the years between Saab-Scania and the Swedish Defense Forces be described in concise terms, illustrating the mutual trust and dependence which has characterized this relationship to the present day? The answer is contained in a letter written in March 1980 by Torsten Rapp, formerly Supreme Commander of the Swedish Armed Forces:

"I received a phone call the other day, asking if I would contribute an historical reminiscence for the Saab-Scania AGM in the middle of April. I agreed with the greatest of pleasure, while expressing my regrets that I should be unable to be present in person on the occasion.

"I should like − both as an airman and a pensioner − to express my great appreciation of being remembered in this manner. As Chief of the Aviation Department of the Swedish Air Force Matériel Administration and, some years later, as Deputy Chief of the Administration itself, I was relatively new to

the collaboration between Saab and the Administration when I arrived on the scene in 1957. Never before had I felt so much at home in a job − a feeling due, in no small part, to our excellent working relationship with Saab − a company which was outstanding in having developed a series of modern aircraft without a single failure, as often happens even the 'major' powers. This was achieved despite the scale of the projects and the concurrent development of more than one aircraft at various times.

"I quickly became aware of the fruitful cooperation which was taking place between Air Force staff, the Administration, research personnel and Saab, all of whom were working together in the truest sense − pulling together unlike their counterparts in some of the bigger countries where the services not only maintained a distance between themselves, but also towards industry.

"I have often said that the outcome of this cooperation − the fact that the best aircraft in the world are of Swedish manufacture — has won us respect abroad, representing, as it does, one of the most persuasive arguments for peace in our overall defense system. This is a thought which a defense minister has at last ventured to articulate.

"I also arrived on the scene at an interesting juncture when the relatively simple 'systems' — airframe, engine and wings — typical of early aircraft were being transformed into complex modern systems by the installation of advanced avionic internals. In this situation, both the electronics industry and the Matériel Administration's electrical experts demanded — and were given — greater influence, including all the extra responsibilities which this entailed. This development created acute problems of demarcation in terms of responsibilities and activities, with all involved seeking to obtain the biggest possible slice of the cake.

"However, to judge from the excellence of the results, the procedures which were adopted proved to be both acceptable and workable by most of the protagonists — truly a unique achievement on the part of Swedish industry.

"The need for cooperation of this nature was abundantly clear. At the most critical stage of the 'struggle', I called the various parties together, using the Book of Books to make this very point. Chapter 12 of Paul's First Letter to the Corinthians contains a passage which describes the most perfectly-designed system of all — man:

'But now they are many members, yet but one body. And the eye cannot say to the hand, I have no need of you; nor again the head to the feet, I have no need of you. And if one member suffers, all the members suffer with it; or if one member be honored, all the members rejoice with it.'

"During my tenure, I have also had the satisfaction of equipping our Defense Forces with missiles. One of my tasks was to eliminate some of the more far-fetched projects then being planned. Another to sign the contracts with the USA and Britain for our first Sidewinder and Bloodhound missiles. I believe that Saab has a vital role to play in the current development of our own ballistic weapons.

"Unfortunately, further advancement prevented me from playing an active role in the administration and coordination of these programs with Saab for longer than three or four years".

Generals Lennart Peyron and Torsten Rapp pictured with Erik Boheman, Chairman of the Saab Board, at the official handover of the last 32B Lansen on 2 May 1960.

1938 — AIRCRAFT PRODUCTION COMMENCES

The new factory was completed in the summer and a license to build the medium-heavy Junkers Ju86K bomber (B3) was won by skillful negotiation on the part of Saab. (Given the imminence of war — which most observers still believed could be averted — it was somewhat surprising that the Germans were prepared to hand over all the plans of one of their most modern bombers.) The design featured a light-alloy fuselage, a type as yet unknown in Sweden. Meticulously designed, it was ideal for series production — for which Saab was provided with complete manufacturing documentation, consisting of no less than 12,000 design drawings, and a complete set of all standard drawings and specifications.

This enabled the Company's designers to concentrate exclusively on modernizing their production methods. Among other measures, no less than 2,000 special tools were made and completely new methods of pressing sheet metal were developed.

Since the main problem was a shortage of skilled labor, "a comprehensive training program was undertaken from the very beginning. As part of the course, the workers were trained in the working of light alloys and familiarized with the concept of aircraft quality" (to quote a local newspaper report). Few suspected that the concept of 'aircraft quality' would later be exploited by Saab to market a completely different product — its cars.

Parliament approved the allocation of an additional SKr 70 million ($23 million) for defense, a substantial proportion being earmarked for the Air Force. Meanwhile, ASJA commenced the manufacture, under license, of a single-engined, light fighter-bomber, the American Northrop 8A-1 (B5). The fact that the first two aircraft built under the auspices of AFF were German and American must, however, be regarded as a coincidence, rather than an expression of Sweden's aspiration of neutrality.

1939 — SWEDEN STANDS PREPARED

Nobody can be sure how well Prime Minister Per-Albin Hansson was briefed when he stated that "Sweden stands prepared". However, he may have been a little more guarded had he known that the Swedish Air Force was equipped with a grand total of 38 heavy bombers, 39 light bombers and 54 fighters.

What quickly became apparent was that all possible resources would have to be committed to building aircraft, and that the 'collaboration' between Saab and ASJA within AFF was completely unworkable in this critical situation. Unwieldy in administrative terms, the joint structure also meant that all investment in plant and machinery had to be duplicated. Tough negotiations finally produced the result on which the Government was really intent, Saab taking over ASJA's operations and AFF being abolished. Torsten Nothin became the Chairman of the Board of the new company, with Ragnar Wahrgren, formerly head of ASJA, as President.

The Trollhättan plant was doubled in size and spacious new design offices were built at Linköping. However, the Government negotiators had been obliged to make substantial concessions as part of the agreement, Saab receiving extensive guarantees as regards future aircraft orders. So generous were these that the press spoke in terms of a monopoly situation, and many observers considered the development to be highly inappropriate.

War broke out on 1 September, and the first Swedish-built B3 was rolled out at Trollhättan only a few weeks later.

However, this essential reinforcement of the understrength Air Force was accompanied by the call-up of large numbers of Company personnel to strengthen the nation's preparedness, forcing both the C-in-C. of the Air Force and Saab management to protest to the Supreme Commander. To quote a contemporary press report: "The legitimate and essential needs of the Air Force and the aircraft industry received a sympathetic hearing, and redress was duly granted, although not as immediately as had been hoped". It may be presumed from this that the workers were exempted from service.

Construction of the control tower at Trollhättan.

1940 – NEW TEETH FOR THE LION

As the Germans occupied Denmark and Norway, and Finland went to war with Russia, the slogan "In this time of crisis, Sweden needs patriotism, vigilance and silence" displayed on a Swedish defense propaganda poster, seemed like something of an understatement. Like a toothless lion, the nation's defense forces were in need of more new teeth like the Saab P7 (B17) which was test-flown in the spring.

Aware of the situation, the RSAF Matériel Administration (acting on behalf of the Government) concluded a framework agreement with Saab and Nohab Flygmotor Fabriker AB, undertaking to purchase equipment worth many million kronor annually. The initial contract was for a total of 16 B3 heavy bombers (actually Ju86s built under license), 102 B5 light bombers (otherwise Northrop 8A1s), 260 P7 (B17) bombers, 88 to 140 P8 (B18) bombers and 200 NA-16-4M trainers (Sk14s built under license). Furthermore, having completed the construction and flight testing of a new fighter (the J21) and a new bomber, Saab was to deliver 210 and 176 of each respective type within 33 months of order by the Administration.

With a span of 22.7 meters (74' 6"), the B3 carried a one-tonne bomb load. Crewed by four men, the aircraft was armed with three swivel-mounted machine guns.

Commenting on the 33-month stipulation, the National Industrial Commission remarked that the time was calculated "from the commencement of design work to the initial delivery of production aircraft", adding that "the production of two new aircraft will provide regular employment for about 600 designers and draftsmen".

The agreement made no reference to prices, confining itself to details of how sales prices and profit margins were to be calculated. The Administration received full access to the Company's accounts for the purpose of monitoring and evaluating all costs. A separate contract was drawn up to cover each stage of delivery in accordance with the conditions of the main agreement, at which point the final price was determined.

It was then open to Saab to rationalize and streamline its production procedures so as to reduce costs and increase its profit margin. These principles were used in all subsequent agreements between the Administration and Saab up to and including the Viggen project.

"Saab gets a flying start!" was the witty headline which appeared in one newspaper of the time.

Carrying a tonne of bombs, the B5 light bomber was armed with one swiveling and four fixed machine guns. The 2-man crew consisted of a pilot and an observer, who also acted as radio-telegraph operator and gunner.

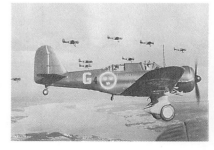

Saab 17

The S17B preserved in the Royal Swedish Air Force museum at Malmslätt.

German standards''. The Americans had never seen these standards, nor could they understand them. Neither, for that matter, could the Swedes since the documents were ''so advanced and highly mathematical that it might just have been possible to use them with the aid of modern computers. It was impossible to decide on an approach; in cases of doubt, we became adept in the art of trial and error''.

Production was under Swedish direction, the Americans being responsible for the drafting work, although ''this could have been undertaken by any one of our shipyards''.

The first test flight took place on 18 May 1940, six months after the end of the American involvement in the project. Not unexpectedly, teething troubles were encountered — the cockpit canopy blew off, spin was difficult to correct and the engine stalled in a right-hand spin (see page 18). However, when the Air Force came to test the plane, they found that ''the aircraft and its equipment are of a generally excellent standard''. A total of 322 aircraft was built in a number of versions equipped with wheels, retractable skids or floats. In service, the plane was known as the S17 or B17 as appropriate (S standing for reconnaissance and B for bomber in Swedish).

The war in Europe also led to the production of the plane as a dive bomber.

Although retired from active operation in 1948, the Saab 17 continued to fly as a target towplane until 1968.

In the late 1930s, ASJA and Saab in Trollhättan (operating under the joint title of AB Förenade Flygverkstäder) competed with each other to build a reconnaissance aircraft for the Swedish Air Force. Although the order went to ASJA, its activities were taken over by Saab in early 1939 and Aircraft 17 became exclusively a Saab project.

Developed in close collaboration with American engineers, the aircraft was a mid-wing monoplane equipped with retractable landing gear. The importance of the American influence has been the subject of controversy, one source maintaining that the ''strength and load distribution calculations were made exclusively by Swedes working to

---

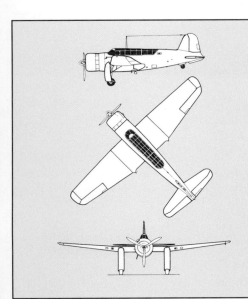

Saab 17

Light bomber and reconnaissance aircraft

Versions	17A, 17B, 17BS, 17C			
Engine type/rating	17A	Pratt & Whitney Twin Wasp/ 1065 hp		
	17B/BS	Bristol Mercury XXIV/980 hp		
	17C	Piaggio PXI bis RC40/1040 hp		

	17A	17B	17BS	17C
Span, m (ft)	13.7 (44'11¼")	13.7 (44'11¼")	13.7 (44'11¼")	13.7 (44'11¼")
Length, m (ft)	9.8 (35'1¾")	9.8 (35'1¾")	9.8 (35'1¾")	9.8 (35'1¾")
Take-off weight, kg (lb)	3790 (8355)	3605 (7948)	3825 (8433)	3870 (8532)
Maximum/cruising speed, km/h	435/390	395/375	330/315	435/370
(mph)	(270/242)	(245/233)	(205/196)	(270/230)
Landing speed, km/h (mph)	125 (77)	125 (77)	125 (77)	125 (77)
Range, km (miles)	1800 (1120)	1400 (870)	2000 (1240)	1700 (1060)
Max. altitude, m (ft)	8700 (28550)	8000 (26250)	6800 (22300)	9800 (32150)

Saab 18

Design work on Aircraft 18, which was destined to become the last propeller-driven military aircraft used by the Swedish Air Force, was commenced at the beginning of 1939.

The Air Force chiefs had announced a competition for the design of a twin-engined aircraft to replace the old B3. The competition − the prize for which was to be the honor and prestige of building the plane − was won by Saab.

"By this time, we had a little experience under our belts and building the plane presented no major problem, even though it was considerably bigger. Everything went like a dream − and everything worked", was the comment of one contemporary spokesman.

The first prototype took to the air on 19 June 1942 under conditions of maximum wartime security. The press was informed merely that the plane "was built from 530 meters of sheet metal, 200,000 rivets, 10 kilometers of electric cable and 600 springs".

Delivered to Bomber Wing F1 in June 1944, the aircraft was designated the B18.

Concentrating mainly on fighters, the Air Force had neglected the need for strategic reconnaissance aircraft. However, following the unusual intermezzo of the Caproni Ca313 (an Italian twin-engined light bomber/reconnaissance craft which suffered from a series of safety problems), several B18s were converted for reconnaissance duties with the installation of radar and camera equipment. This version became known as the S18A.

The first B18B flew on 10 June 1944. With new engines, this version was one of the fastest piston-engined aircraft in the world, reaching a top speed of 570 km/h (354 mph).

Yet another version, the T18B, could either be fitted with torpedoes for anti-shipping duties or armed with a single 157-mm and two 20-mm automatic cannons.

Production of the Saab 18 ended in 1949 when 242 planes had been built. The last of these was retired from active service in 1959.

Apart from rivets and bolts, a B18 consisted of about 15,000 components. The crew had something like 160 levers, controls and buttons to operate and 45 instruments to read.

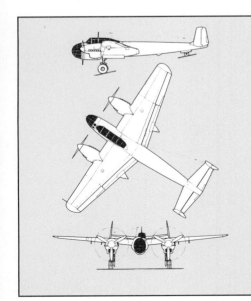

Saab 18

Medium-heavy bomber, strike and long-distance reconnaissance aircraft

Versions	B/S18A, B18B, T18B		
Engine type/rating	A	Pratt & Whitney Twin Wasp/1065 hp	
	B	Daimler Benz 605B/1475 hp	

	B/S18A	B18B	T18B
Span, m (ft)	17.04 (55'10¾")	17.04 (55'10¾")	17.04 (55'10¾")
Length, m (ft)	13.23 (43'4¾")	13.23 (43'4¾")	13.23 (43'4¾")
Take-off weight, kg (lb)	8700 (1918)	8793 (1938)	9272 (2044)
Maximum/cruising speed, km/h	465/415	570/480	595/480
mph	(289/258)	(354/298)	(370/298)
Landing speed, km/h (mph)	135 (84)	125 (78)	130 (81)
Range, km (miles)	2200 (1367)	2600 (1616)	2600 (1616)
Max. altitude, m (ft)	8000 (26250)	9800 (32150)	9300 (30150)

Daredevils of the skies — the test pilots

The four photographs on these pages were taken by Lennart Nilsson for the photo-magazine 'Se' in the 40s. Like Captain Claes Smith, a test pilot of the time was expected to look like Errol Flynn in 'Dive Bomber' (a 1941 movie).

The moment of truth — the maiden flight of a B18. Nobody knows for certain how the plane will behave!

Captain Claes Smith — one of the original test pilots — has provided a graphic account of test flying in the early pioneering days:

"I made my first test flight for the Company on the afternoon of the day I arrived in Trollhättan. The plane was the first Swedish-assembled B3. No test reports were available; in fact, the aircraft had neither been finished nor undergone full ground testing. As an example, the landing gear could not be retracted. However, the main object was to get it airborne and to see if it behaved more or less normally. And it did!

"My next assignment was to fly the Sk14 and B5, both of which were built under license at Linköping. Since these two planes were proven types, test flights consisted largely of simple production 'flight checks' in which the items listed on four fairly straight-forward sheets were ticked off as the checks were made. A great deal of attention (unwarranted, in our opinion) was devoted to spin. Every production Sk14 had to be tested at both extremes of the permissible center of gravity range in both right and left-hand spins. This was, perhaps, more a test of the pilot's coordination than of the aircraft's capabilities. Having stabilized the spin after a number of rolls, the 'dive angle', rate of spin and altitude loss per roll were observed and recorded. The air speed indicators were calibrated by flying a triangular course. Finally, the plane was flown upside-down for some minutes with the engine canopy open to empty out any debris, rivets or even tools which had been left behind, to prevent them from interfering with the control cables and other mechanisms.

"Adjustments required to correct or improve the flying characteristics were carried out subsequently by the test pilot in cooperation with the mechanics. The design and planning departments were consulted if a modification was considered necessary by the pilot.

"Parachutes were the only special equipment we had — I had bought my own winter flying kit during my time in the Air Force. Flight observations were made on a 'knee-pad' consisting of a roll of paper scrounged from any of the office girls who happened to have a calculator.

"The outbreak of the War complicated flight testing arrangements, particularly at Trollhättan. On the very first day, all cars were commandeered and used to block the runways to potential enemies. The cars were subsequently replaced by wooden trestles which were moved in accordance with a pre-determined pattern to provide space for taking off and landing. The anti-aircraft batteries in the neighborhood were another problem. For production reasons, every plane was painted with a green primer, and although army command was notified of every flight, the gunners often mistook us for Germans and let fly. The first three rounds were warning shots. However, when the first black salvo appeared, rapid evasive action quickly became part of the test. It might have been helpful if incidents of this type could have been reported by radio. However, although we carried the equipment, we were forbidden to use it — Saab was a civilian outfit and radio was a state monopoly! In the fullness of time, closer liaison was established with the technicians at the Flight Test Center at Malmslätt, including consultation in working out the flight schedules.

"Customer specifications at the time were fairly basic. Testing was generally a matter of confirming that the plane was capable of its design performance and that its flying qualities were satisfactory, also that it could withstand the maximum design stresses. The weapons were tested for satisfactory operation and – a factor which was still considered highly important – the ability of the plane to recover normally from a spin was verified. The speed and simplicity of ground servicing were checked at the drawing-board stage.

"The new airfield had not been completed in time for the first test flight of the B17, a 600-meter (1,970 ft) runway in between the buildings being used for take-off. Since radio communication was still prohibited, we were forced to use an Air Force plane as a tracker to provide visual observation of anything abnormal. The method has its drawbacks. For example, the observers failed to note that the canopy on one B17 opened during take-off. Although I tried to hang on to it, I needed both hands for landing and had no choice but to let it go. The piece landed in a meadow from which we subsequently recovered it.

"As part of the performance tests designed to verify the plane's climbing and speed capabilities, I installed Saab's first test-flight instrument, a 4:50 kronor thermometer which was provided with a cover and mounted on one of the wings, where it showed the outside air temperature somewhat more accurately than the ordinary gauge.

"Some parameters could not be recorded at all. For example, the J21 was the first aircraft to be fitted with an accelerometer with twin indicators, one of which continuously displayed the maximum value reached during the test.

"Spin tests on the B17 gave trouble from the start. The engine stalled when the plane entered a spin and the spin itself was difficult to correct. The latter problem was identified by fitting a series of woolen streamers to the tail fin and rudder, enabling the observer in a tracker plane to confirm that 75% of the surfaces were in a turbulent air flow at full rudder during the spin. The solution was to fit a small extra fin under the tail.

"The ground communications problems were solved when the Company purchased a ground station, which it donated to the Air Force and operated as a military installation staffed by its own personnel. Since we transmitted on short wave, the severe interference and primitive technology made telephonic communications extremely unreliable. As a result, important messages were always sent by telegraph.

"In the case of prototypes, the Saab pilot flew a test (or a series of tests), following which the same program was repeated by a pilot from the Test Center at Malmslätt on behalf of the Air Force. This was an impractical method, given the scarcity of aviation fuel which existed during this period of crisis. As a result, every second test flight of a plane with two or more seats was made with the other pilot as observer and recorder – a system which worked excellently.

"The military aircraft which succeeded the J21 were jet-powered. I was anxious to travel to England to familiarize myself with these engines. However, after looking at the costs, Company management decided it would be less expensive to bring over a British pilot to train me.

"Work on the Saab Scandia commenced shortly afterwards and occupied all my time. By then, codes governing both the design and testing of commercial aircraft had been introduced in the USA. With the adoption of the American rules by most of the world's civil aviation authorities and their introduction as part of the Scandia test program, the 'pioneering days' were obviously numbered".

Test Pilot Anders Helgstrand had little time to make notes on his kneepad during the flight.

'Tandem flying' was adopted to save flying time. During the test flight, the observer occupied the gunner's position.

Assembly of the B17 in Linköping. On average, one plane was built every three days. The resemblance to modern assembly plants is striking.

1941 — THE FIRST SAAB-DESIGNED AIRCRAFT

In March, the RSAF Matériel Administration requested Saab to submit a design proposal for a new fighter. Only a month later, representatives of the Administration were invited by the Company to view an airplane unique in Swedish aviation history — an all-metal monoplane with twin tail booms, designed by Frid Wänström. Since nothing like this had ever been seen in Sweden before, the Air Force was skeptical, to say the least. However, the Saab engineers had confidence in the design and, after a brief flirtation with a more conventional model, the Air Force gave its assent.

Apparently considering its 1939 commitments to have been too generous, the Administration sought to relinquish its agreement with Saab, only to meet with the Board's refusal. To strengthen its hand, the Air Force had developed its own design of fighter; however, its own experts considered the production plans over-ambitious and the project was abandoned. A direct inquiry as to whether Saab would undertake to produce the aircraft was rejected, despite the risk that this might lead the Administration to reconsider its own plans — a step which would obviously be detrimental to the Company. Nevertheless, the critics maintained — and Saab's engineers were quick to see — that if Saab was to build a fighter which was not of the highest quality, the Company (to quote the minutes of a Board meeting) "would be held responsible by the public for the poor quality of the product and its reputation severely damaged".

In October, the Supreme Commander visited the Linköping and Trollhättan plants, and was obviously impressed to the extent of promising to "reinforce the anti-aircraft defenses to protect the installations" and undertaking to ensure that "Company personnel will not be called up for military service".

Production of the Saab 17 proceeded as planned, the first production model being delivered in December.

The problems of releasing the bombs from the Saab 17 were described by a pilot in the following graphic terms: "Whether or not the bombs fell was occasionally a matter of pure chance; the system was new and untried. Failure was likely to draw the unmistakable wrath of wing command: 'Don't give me excuses; the Air Force can do it. Just drop the ***** things!' All you could do then was to pull the crate harder out of the dive — even if the wing struts began to crumple".

Torsten Nothin
Chairman of Svenska Aeroplan
AB, 1939—1958

1942 — A THREAT TO SURVIVAL

A National Defense Committee report published at the beginning of the year proposed that the Swedish Air Force be organized into 16 wings, operating a total of 957 aircraft which were to be replaced over a 7-year period. In other words, 140 new planes would be required annually. However, the Committee also recommended that production of the replacement aircraft should preferably be shared by several manufacturers — a proposal which was in direct conflict with the Government's stated policy of negotiating with a single supplier. Following protests by the Saab Board, this proposal was rejected.

The first prototype of the Saab 18 — a twin-engined dive bomber and reconnaissance aircraft which Design Department had been working on since 1939 — made its maiden flight in the summer. Since the rate of production was now such that skilled aircraft workers were in short supply, the Board decided, at the suggestion of President Ragnar Wahrgren, to establish an engineering trades school as a means of recruiting workers and future foremen. The school was to provide a 4-year course with 15 students in each year. Selected with great care, the trainees were obliged by contract to complete the course. As an additional incentive, each was credited with a one-off payment of SKr 120 ($40) plus 2 öre (0.7 cents) per hour — payable only when the course had been completed and the contract fulfilled. Fourteen to sixteen was considered to be the appropriate entry age. The program became the origin of a training philosophy which has exemplified the Company's personnel policies ever since.

1943 — A SERIOUS INCIDENT

Frid Wänström had completed the preliminary design of his creation, the J21, in ten days, and the time had now come for the aircraft's maiden flight.

Wänström tells the tale in his memoirs: "The flight was to take place on 30 July, following some taxiing tests on the ground. However, when the time came to take off, the plane refused to lift. It continued its run and lifted only at the last second, just avoiding a ditch. The landing gear struck a fence and we had to belly-land at Malmslätt. Being a project engineer was no fun at that time!" However, the design was not to blame. Wänström continues: "As luck would have it, we soon discovered the cause — the brakes had remained on. Imagine if the plane had crashed during its first flight and we had been unable to find the reason! To give us a longer runway, the 21 was shipped to Såtenäs on a canal barge and things went better next time".

Although the Air Force had ordered 60 Sk14s, the order had (perhaps by good fortune) been received before the J21 'demonstration'. Whether or not the official representatives would have overlooked the human factor and retained their faith in Saab, the design of the J21 was in no way at fault. This major order necessitated further expansion of the Trollhättan plant.

K.G. Fritzsche seen riveting a spar to a wing rib using a stationary riveter.

Checking the assembled B18 engines prior to mounting on the bulkhead.

Saab 21

Frid Wänström, leader of the Saab 17 project and later Head of Research, was involved in the development of all aircraft up to the 37 Viggen. In 1948, he and A.J. Andersson, another Saab employee, received the Thulin Medal for aeronautical research.

On 1 April 1939, the Air Force Matériel Administration invited AB Förenade Flygverkstäder to tender for a new fighter aircraft to be powered by the new Bristol Taurus engine, a sleeve-valve unit delivering 1,200 hp. The timetable was incredibly tight. The final tender was to be submitted by 15 July, a prototype was to be built by 1 July 1941 and full-scale production was to commence exactly two years later. Designer Frid Wänström completed the preliminary design in 10 days. As luck would have it, he lived within a 10-minute walk of his office and was able to snatch a short nap on his couch every day. Summing up the results of his efforts, Wänström remarked: "Even now, I still don't understand how I did it".

Saab proposed a radical configuration (designated the L13) in which the engine was mounted behind the cockpit, offering the advantages of a twin-engined craft in terms of visibility and armament. Unfortunately, this proved to be impractical since the Taurus engine was air-cooled.

Meanwhile, the Air Force solved its fighter problems by importing J9s and by continuing to produce its own J22s. However, the position became critical when imports were interrupted by the war and, in March 1941, Saab was authorized to resume work on the fighter project. By this time, technology had outstripped the original L13 concept and a new liquid-cooled Daimler-Benz engine was available as though made to order. The modified design − the J21 − was presented to the Air Force chiefs on 1 April 1941.

However, problems remained to be solved − an obvious one being that the pilot was likely to be cut to pieces by the propeller if forced to bail out. After discussions as to the feasibility of jettisoning either the propeller or the complete engine, it was decided to opt for the safer and less expensive alternative of ejecting the pilot. As a result, the J21 became one of the first aircraft ever to be equipped with an ejection seat.

Despite the new engine, cooling problems persisted and the test aircraft carried a large hay-drying fan which supplied extra air through special hoses to the wing air intakes.

Nevertheless, the first prototype made its maiden flight on 30 July 1943, and the first operational aircraft was delivered to F8 Wing at Barkaby on 1 December 1945. Continuous improvements were made and a bomb-carrying version, the J21A-3, made its debut on 22 May 1947. Although increasing the speed was the first priority of the plane's designers at this time, all attempts to achieve this aim using piston engines were abandoned with the advent of the jet engine in late 1945, and four J21A-1s were modified in an initial attempt to adopt the new technology. However, the redesign proved much more extensive than was first envisaged, affecting 50% of the airframe rather than 20% as had been anticipated. In hindsight, the J21R which emerged from the project must be regarded as something less than a success, although it did provide experience which was to prove valuable to the Company in its own jet engine development work. Saab built a total of 64 of this particular version.

To bridge the gap between the J21R and the J29 (the next jet, which was already at the design stage), the RSAF imported British Vampire J28s equipped with the same Goblin engine as the J21R. To make way for the new

The J21, showing the distinctive twin tail-boom configuration.

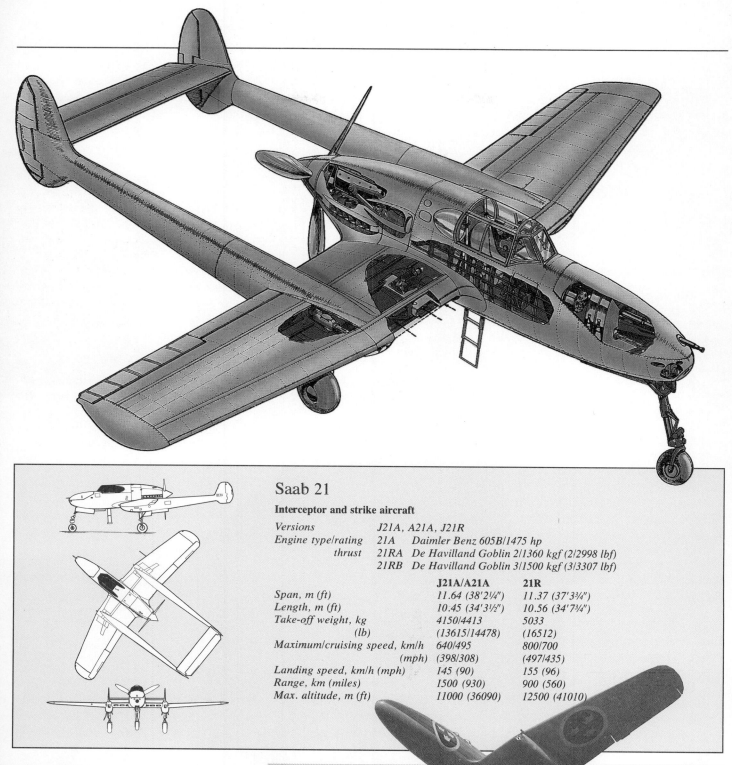

Saab 21

Interceptor and strike aircraft

Versions	J21A, A21A, J21R	
Engine type/rating	21A	Daimler Benz 605B/1475 hp
thrust	21RA	De Havilland Goblin 2/1360 kgf (2/2998 lbf)
	21RB	De Havilland Goblin 3/1500 kgf (3/3307 lbf)

	J21A/A21A	21R
Span, m (ft)	11.64 (38'2¼")	11.37 (37'3¾")
Length, m (ft)	10.45 (34'3½")	10.56 (34'7¾")
Take-off weight, kg	4150/4413	5033
(lb)	(13615/14478)	(16512)
Maximum/cruising speed, km/h	640/495	800/700
(mph)	(398/308)	(497/435)
Landing speed, km/h (mph)	145 (90)	155 (96)
Range, km (miles)	1500 (930)	900 (560)
Max. altitude, m (ft)	11000 (36090)	12500 (41010)

aircraft, the number of J21Rs was reduced from 120 to 60. A complete series was abandoned, and enough wings, bodies and other components to equip an entire wing were scrapped.

In all, 298 J21s were built. The last of these was retired from service on 23 July 1954, although the J21R continued to fly until 4 April 1957.

The J21R was the first Swedish jet built for the Swedish Air Force. The plane also became the only propeller-powered aircraft to have been converted to jet propulsion and produced in series.

Saab 90 Scandia

The Scandia was the first civil airliner produced by the Swedish aviation industry.

Although the defense chiefs wanted the new aircraft to be a combined airliner and bomber (like the B3), a compromise proposed by the Swedish airline, AB Aerotransport (ABA) — which was expected to be the main customer — was adopted, and the Scandia was designed for conversion into a troop carrier in the event of war.

28 February 1944 — the date on which the Board of Saab took the decision to proceed with the project — might be said to be the Scandia's birthday.

The objective was to build a short-haul aircraft with an ideal combination of low-speed maneuverability and low landing speed to minimize take-off and landing distances — features designed to maximize punctuality and air safety (regardless of weather) in those countries expected to buy the plane. With a range of 1,000 kilometers (621 miles), the Scandia was to carry 25—30 passengers.

The results of the first test flight, on 16 November 1946, were sufficient to encourage ABA to sign a contract for 10 aircraft at a value of SKr 15 million ($5 million). The first plane was delivered in October 1950.

In the shadow of the cold war, however, the J29 project was considered to be of higher priority, and production of the Scandia was transferred to Fokker in 1951, Saab receiving compensation from the Swedish Air Force for the abandonment of the project. At this point, the Company had delivered 8 aircraft to ABA and exported 10 to Brazil. In time, the ABA planes were also sold to Brazil, where they remained in service until 1969.

The year was 1944. War would soon be over, borders thrown open and people would take to the air. Buoyed by the spirit of optimism engendered by this prospect, Saab embarked on two civil aircraft projects — the Saab 90 Scandia, a twin-engined airliner, and the Saab 91 Safir, a single-engined trainer and private plane.

Tord Lidmalm led the Saab 90 Scandia project and managed the design office. Until his retirement, he was Technical Director of the Saab-Scania Group.

Saab 90A-2 Scandia

Commercial airliner, 24—32 passengers

	90A-2	
Engine type/rating		Pratt & Whitney Twin Wasp R-2180/1825 hp
Span, m (ft)		28.0 (91'10½")
Length, m (ft)		21.3 (69'10½")
Take-off weight, kg (lb)		15900 (35053)
Maximum/cruising speed, km/h (mph)		455/400 (283/249)
Landing speed, km/h (mph)		120 (75)
Range, km (miles)		2650 (1650)
Max. altitude, m (ft)		8700 (28540)

Saab 91 Safir

Safety was the keynote of the Safir. Design work was started in Winter 1944–45 and the first prototype – a 3-seater model with a Gypsy Major 147-hp engine and a top speed of 265 km/h (165 mph) – took to the air on 20 November 1945.

Series production commenced in Spring 1946, 48 aircraft being built between then and 1950. Ten of these were bought by the Swedish Air Force for liaison and light transport duties. The 91B, with a 190-hp engine and a top speed of 275 km/h (171 mph), was introduced in 1949. This model (which was also used as a trainer from 1952 on) was followed by a 4-seater version designated the 91C.

The 91D – the last of the series – was equipped with a new, lighter, 180-hp engine.

In all, 323 Safirs were built for delivery to 21 countries and 6 air forces, making the aircraft the Company's most successful export in the aviation field.

The Saab 201 and 202 deserve passing mention as curiosities. Actually Safirs fitted with half-sized J29 and A32 wings, these were used for aerodynamic research which was to prove invaluable in the development of the latter two aircraft.

The Swedish Air Force operated ninety Saab 91 Safirs under the designation Sk50.

A.J. Andersson started his career as a designer with Bücker in Germany. Later Saab's Chief Designer, his creations included the Saab 91 Safir.

Safir 91A, serial No. 3, was delivered to Uno Ranch of Gothenburg in 1946. He is still flying the plane more than 40 years later!

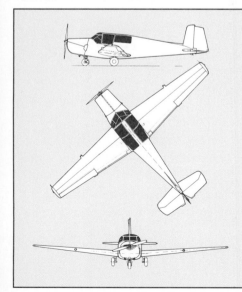

Saab 91 Safir

Executive, sports and training aircraft

Versions	91A, 91B, 91C and 91D		
Engine type/rating	91A	De Havilland Gipsy Major X/147 hp	
	91B/C	Lycoming 435A/190 hp	
	91D 80	Lycoming 360A1A/180 hp	

	91A	91B/C	91D
Span, m (ft)	10.6 (34'9¼")	10.6 (34'9¼")	10.6 (34'9¼")
Length, m (ft)	7.80 (25'10¼")	7.95 (26'1")	8.03 (26'4½")
Take-off weight, kg (lb)	1075 (2370)	1215 (2472)	1205 (2657)
Maximum/cruising speed, km/h (mph)	265/248 (165/154)	275/240 (171/149)	270/235 (168/146)
Landing speed, km/h (mph)	85 (53)	90 (56)	90 (56)
Range, km (miles)	960 (597)	1075 (668)	1060 (659)
Max. altitude, m (ft)	4600 (15090)	6200 (20340)	6100 (20010)

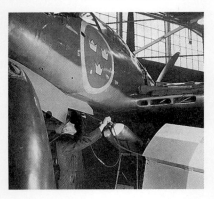

Filling a pilot's oxygen bottles. The oxygen mask was connected to a supply point on a side panel in the cockpit.

1944 – PEACE ON THE HORIZON

As the end of the war approached, it became obvious that Saab's military contracts would no longer be sufficient to keep its specialized workforce in employment. Although production capacity was fully booked until 1947, the absence of new orders from the Matériel Administration led to the redundancy of about 70 employees in the design department.

The only alternative was to seek a foothold in the civilian sector, the first step in this direction being an order for the conversion of five American 'Flying Fortresses' which had made an emergency landing in Sweden. Although the planes were relatively uneconomic and carried only 14 passengers, the Swedish airline, AB Aerotransport (ABA), proposed to use them as passenger planes. The modifications, which were required to enable ABA to fly the Atlantic, provided the Saab engineers with invaluable experience.

Although the Company was well to the fore in the field and optimism was high, Erik Rydberg, Plant Manager at Trollhättan, expressed himself in somewhat pessimistic terms in a newspaper interview: "As far as the industry in Sweden is concerned, it is quite clear that the new 'jet plane' will not be suitable for passenger services or, indeed, freight operations. Here in Sweden, we must keep our feet on the ground, even where flying is concerned".

However, Rydberg was more realistic in his prophecy that "the Swedish aircraft industry is likely to enjoy exactly the same prospects of success as other quality-oriented Swedish industries when it comes to competing with its finished aircraft in the international postwar market".

Design Department was allocated SKr 200,000 ($70,000) by the Board for the development of a civil airliner. According to the minutes, "Mr. Wallenberg remarked that he considered the proposal to be fraught with risk. For example, Aerotransport would find it very easy after the war to purchase American aircraft such as the DC-3 to meet its requirements for several years ahead". As on so many other occasions, events were to prove him right!

1945 – CRISIS

It appeared as though Saab's collaboration with the Matériel Administration might also produce results in the civilian sector. With financial support from the state investment fund, the production of a high-quality passenger plane would support operations during the next few critical years until 1950. Designed for conversion into a military transport, the plane would also be attractive to the Defense Forces which, in peacetime, could lease a number of them to ABA. Despite its appeal, the idea fell through when the Air Force announced that it considered the project more appropriate to the Swedish Army.

Other proposals to safeguard employment were submitted in an internal report, the products suggested being as diverse as spinning reels and prefabricated sheet steel warehouse buildings. However, the SKr 200,000 ($70,000) already allocated for the development of a civil airliner bore fruit and, following the approval of additional funding, the first aircraft, known as the Safir, duly made its inaugural flight.

However, the Safir alone was not sufficient to fill the vacuum left by the fall-off in military orders, and President Ragnar Wahrgren reported to a Board meeting that "the Company has examined the feasibility of making cars". DKW had sold considerable numbers of cars before the war and this market was now more or less open. A front-wheel-drive, 2-cycle model costing about SKr 3,200 ($1,100) would probably be the right product, while an annual output of 2,500 to 3,000 cars would match the capacity of the Trollhättan plant. Using its experience of aircraft aerodynamics, Design Department undertook to increase the car's acceleration by 50% compared with the DKW. Adjudging the project worthwhile, the Board allocated SKr 200,000 ($70,000) for development work.

1946 – PROJECT 'SMALL CAR'

The Scandia, which flew for the first time in November after an unusually short development period, was the first airliner to be built. ABA (the Swedish national airline at the time) being the natural customer, its engineers had cooperated with Saab in its design.

Although the airline bought a number of Scandias, the employment situation continued to be critical, and the question now was whether the car project could save Trollhättan. The Board was divided on the matter, some members arguing that contract work should be sought from other industries to maintain the plant in production. However, this proposal was rejected.

Project 'Small Car' was pursued, the specifications of the proposed model emerging by degrees. Front-wheel drive (then a relatively unproven design) was to be a major selling point, especially under Swedish climatic conditions. Among other advantages, most of the mechanical components would be mounted in one location, leaving the rest of the space for passengers and baggage.

Estimates showed that at a price of SKr 3,900 ($1,300), "all of the initial development costs should be recouped when 8,000 cars have been sold".

The project became even more urgent when the Air Force announced that it had been offered 50 to 60 Mustang fighters at SKr 20,000 ($7,000) each by a supplier in the USA, and that it proposed to halve the order for J21s to 240 aircraft – a proposal which would have closed the Trollhättan plant within six months. However, following representations by Company management, the parties agreed to a reduction of 62 aircraft, the Air Force paying for the materials already purchased to build the planes.

The next piece of bad news came a few months later when the C-in-C. sought permission to buy 200 Sk16s from abroad at a price as low as SKr 10,000 ($3,500) each. Although Saab was building the Sk14 under license, it was obliged to approve the purchase under the terms of the agreement.

Although a formal decision to undertake the production of cars was yet to be made, a sum of SKr 800,000 ($270,000) was allocated for the manufacture of three test models, with a further SKr 600,000 ($200,000) for the purchase of presses. At the same time, the Board proposed that the Company should enter into negotiations with the Government with a view to securing a guaranteed return from car production, since the survival of Trollhättan was essential in terms of national preparedness.

It may have been the rumors of crisis which encouraged Svenska Flygmotor AB to inquire confidentially "whether the Company's premises at Trollhättan, with the exception of the hangar and airfield, but including machinery and inventories not designed specifically for aircraft manufacture, might be acquired at book value". The answer was no!

The prototype of the Saab 92 took less than 6 months to build in 1946. Although many parts were borrowed from other cars, the final shape is recognizable. The lines had been finalized by the time the second test model was built.

Saab 92

Made entirely by hand, the prototype of the 92 (the original Saab) was so well built that it still looks spick-and-span today, many arduous kilometers and forty years later.

The people of Sweden caught their first glimpse of a Saab car on 10 June 1947 when the first prototype of the 92002 design was shown to the assembled press at Linköping.

The journalists were told that the car was equipped with front-wheel drive and possessed "superb handling qualities". The pure aerodynamic shape — the result of wind tunnel testing at the National Swedish Aeronautical Research Institute — contributed to "minimizing the power demand and fuel consumption". Top speed was said to be 100 km/h (62 mph). The transversely-mounted engine was a 2-cylinder, 2-cycle unit with a rating of 25 hp.

It had been a long and arduous road!

Preliminary design work had been commenced in late 1945 when company management decided to undertake the manufacture of a car in an attempt to diversify its product

Although the design of the instrument panel was not of the same high standard as the body, it was adequate for the purposes of test driving.

In 1946, the divided rear window was not regarded as being unusually small.

By the time the second prototype – Saab 92002 – was built, the car had already acquired its final shape from designer Sixten Sason (below).

range, the general assumption being that sales of military aircraft would fall with the achievement of world peace.

The first body designs were completed in January 1946 and a full-scale wooden model was built. Following considerable modification, the model was finished on 15 April, manual production of an actual body having been started a couple of weeks earlier. The work was carried out by a sheet metal craftsman who used a block of oak placed on a pile of horse manure to achieve just the right resiliency! The car – shining black and streamlined – was completed in Summer 1946, the engine, transmission and a variety of other mechanical components having been procured from various scrapyards.

Truth to tell, the original Saab – which bore the designation 92001 – was neither a particularly attractive nor practical car. However, the unrelenting round-the-clock testing to which it was subjected yielded invaluable experience which was fully utilized when building the second prototype (92002) – in appearance, a considerably more elegant car. So elegant, in fact, was this design that it came to characterize the entire Saab range for the next 30 years. Saab 92002 was completed in May 1947.

A third prototype was built before the entire production operation was transferred to Trollhättan. In all, the three models underwent endurance testing over a total of 280,000 kilometers (174,000 miles).

Sales in Sweden were to be handled by Philipsons Automobil AB, who ordered no less than 8,000 cars and made a major financial contribution to the project by paying for a third in advance. However, Philipsons also expressed some reservations about the design, as a result of which an inexpensive

The Saab 92 was unmistakably the work of an airplane designer. With its round shape and sweeping aerodynamic lines, it resembled no other car yet built.

Appearing in 1953, the Saab 92B boasted a proper trunk — and all Saabs were no longer bottle-green! The engine rating was increased from 25 to 28 hp in the 1954 model.

Saab 92, 1950—1956

2-door Sedan

Length/width/height: 395/162/145 cm (156/64/ 57 in)
Two-cylinder, 2-cycle, 764-cm³, 25-hp, transversely mounted engine
Three-speed transmission with freewheel and column-mounted gearshift
Independent suspension, torsion bars front and rear
Drum brakes all round with parking brake acting on rear wheels
Top speed: approx. 105 km/h (65 mph)

basic version was deleted from the range; all of the cars were to be de luxe models.

The 92 suffered from a number of drawbacks. Among other oddities, it did not have a trunk, and baggage had to be stowed from the rear seat. Other problems included poor visibility to the rear and a tendency for the engine to overheat. Nevertheless, despite its peculiarities, the car became a success and prospective buyers soon began to form long queues.

All beginnings are hard — and the 92's was no exception. Although the design was steadily improved, it took considerably longer

The 2-cylinder, 2-cycle engine was a compact design. The power train occupied only a small proportion of the space, leaving the remainder for the occupants and their baggage. Comparison with the design philosophy of the Saab 9000 is interesting.

than expected to develop the necessary production facilities. Not until Summer 1949 was an initial series of 20 cars built on a mass production scale, production proper beginning in the middle of December. Starting with an output of 3, and then 4 cars per day, the plant nevertheless achieved a production of 1,248 cars — all practically identical — by the end of 1950. The Company had obviously taken to heart the sales pitch used by another famous manufacturer — Ford — who promised their customers any color they wanted provided it was black. The only difference was that the 92s were green.

The extremely high proportion of Swedish components and materials was an interesting aspect. Imported parts accounted for only 17% of the cost.

Ideally designed for tortuous roads, the 92 had competed in several minor rallies in the west of Sweden by December 1949. With its completely flat underside, the car coped easily with uneven surfaces, while the pure aerodynamic shape was a further advantage. And, only one month after the start of production, the cars bearing chassis Nos. 7 and 8 were entered in the Monte Carlo Rally, finishing in 55th and 69th places (see page 42).

Only minor changes were made during the initial years of manufacture, the 1953 model being the first to undergo modification to the extent that it warranted the addition of a 'B' to the type designation. At this point, 5,300 92s had already been built — all finished in the same standard color which had now become somewhat of a Saab trademark. Innovations on the 1953 model included a larger rear window, a trunk, a removable rear seat, transfer of the battery to the engine compartment and — at long last — a choice of colors.

By the time car No. 10,000 left the plant on 6 March 1954, output was running at one car every 27 minutes — nearly four times the initial rate four years earlier. Demand continued at an extremely high level and, following the opening of a new plant in Gothenburg, 6,000 cars per annum were produced up to the end of 1956. In December 1955 the model's successor — the Saab 93 — was unveiled.

In terms of technical achievement, the Saab 92 and Saab J21 represented something of a pinnacle in the late 1940s.

Saab exported 48 cars during the first two years of production, nearly half of them to Denmark. The first car exported to the USA was shipped as early as 1951.

Gunnar Ljungström (below) and Sixten Sason worked as a team to create the first Saab car. Sason ensured that Ljungström's technical concepts were elegantly 'packaged'.

1947 — A NEW ELEMENT

Although Project 'Small Car' was the major event of the year, it is worth noting that Saab also established itself in a completely new element. As part of its diversification program, the Company manufactured a series of 250 aluminum rowboats, some of which were sold to Africa. Since the Stångån river was frozen, the prototype was tested in the Tannefors School swimming pool.

The car project gave rise to several heated boardroom debates centering on the preservation of employment at Trollhättan. Closure was likely to make the designers redundant, while other skilled workers would seek employment elsewhere. This would make it impossible for the Company to fulfill its future contracts with the Matériel Administration (some members of which were already recommending that future aircraft should be purchased from abroad).

In this situation, voices were heard to propose that Flygmotor's offer to buy the plant should be reconsidered as the only means of enabling car production to go ahead.

Another proposal came from Philipsons Automobil AB offering a contract to purchase 8,000 cars (a total of three years' production) in a single deal, a major proportion of the purchase price to be paid in advance to finance production. After this, the decision-making process became a formality.

The first Saab was unveiled to the public at a press showing in Linköping. Although the car was not due for production until a couple of years later, prospective buyers began to queue for it immediately following the successful launching.

Meanwhile, the aircraft designers were busy with the new technology of jet propulsion and the first Swedish-built jet plane — the Saab 21R (a refined version of the J21) — was test-flown for the first time.

Having recommended the Ethiopian Air Force to purchase a number of Safirs, Count Carl von Rosen demonstrated that they had made the correct choice by flying one of the planes non-stop from Stockholm to Addis Ababa (a distance of 6,220 kilometers or 3,865 miles) in a world record time of 30 1/2 hours.

Designer Kurt Sjögren and his colleagues during the first test of a hydrofoil prototype which never entered production.

The jet engine

In the jet engine, air is drawn in through the intake at the front and compressed, producing a rise in temperature. The hot air is then mixed with the fuel (aviation kerosene). Ignited when the engine is started, combustion of the mixture then becomes self-sustaining. The hot exhaust gases are discharged through a nozzle at the rear of the engine, producing a reactive force which propels the aircraft forward. The gases are also used to drive the turbine which powers the compressor and air-intake fan.

The press showing of the Saab 92 took place on 10 June 1947 in the staff club at Linköping. The blue-black model bore the chassis number 92.002.

1948 – RENEWED AGREEMENT

The agreement with the Matériel Administration expired – and there is reason to believe that sighs of relief were heaved in the boardroom when it was renewed until 1958.

The delivery schedule specified in the new agreement was based on the assumption that the matériel requirements of the scaled-down Air Force proposed by the National Defense Committee in 1945 would be renewed. Saab was also to be prepared to increase production under certain circumstances, while the Administration was to be entitled to reduce the level of orders placed with the Company subject to "appropriate financial compensation".

Another reason for slow delivery which the Administration was certain to find unacceptable was the fact that the Trollhättan airfield became a morass in fall and spring, causing planes to sink to their wheel hubs in a sea of mud. The solution was the construction of a 600-m (1,970 ft) surfaced runway at a cost of SKr 2.3 million ($0.5 million).

ABA signed a contract for 10 Scandias worth SKr 15 million ($3 million), while combined demonstration and sales trips were made to Norway, Ireland, Scotland, England, Denmark, the Netherlands and Belgium in further efforts to sell the plane.

Jet propulsion and supersonic flight – the two latest areas of aviation technology – required specialists who were in short supply. To alleviate the scarcity, Saab introduced courses designed to improve the qualifications of some of its engineers to degree level in certain subjects. Although the first course attracted 80 applicants, only 20 places were, unfortunately, available.

1949 – YOUR MONEY OR YOUR LIFE

The machines stood ready. A skilled and well-trained force of assembly workers waited... and continued to wait. In postwar Sweden, foreign trade was subject to strict state controls, and the Government had refused Saab the foreign currency which it needed to purchase materials from the USA, Britain, Germany and Czechoslovakia, advising it to conclude barter deals instead. However, since the Company possessed neither the time nor the expertise to indulge in this activity, it approached the Ministry of Industry directly with its demands.

The restrictions were eventually lifted, although not completely, the Government having its own views on the pricing of the car. The National Price Control Board stipulated that the model should be sold for SKr 5,500 ($1,100) to dealers and SKr 6,500 ($1,300) to retail buyers.

In reality, the position was still so precarious that 'Stockholms Tidningen' reported: "It is high time that the Government produced a policy for the aircraft industry. If it wishes to promote an independent Swedish industry, it must assist Saab in selling the Scandia airliner. Should the company fail in this endeavor, it will have no further opportunity of building aircraft other than those ordered by the Air Force".

In spite of all, the first production car eventually left the works, by which time Philipsons had an impressive list of orders. An innovation was the establishment of works councils at the Linköping and Trollhättan plants. As originally constituted, these consisted of seven management, three white-collar and seven blue-collar representatives who met on a quarterly basis.

The entrance to the new underground premises at Linköping which housed machine shops, goods reception and inspection facilities, as well as locker rooms, washrooms and two canteens. The temperature variation was ± 1°C and the premises were supplied with 120 m³/h (4,240 ft³/h) of fresh air per occupant.

Final assembly of the J21R.

Saab 29 'Tunnan'

The 'Flying Barrel' was armed with rockets and bombs, in addition to four fixed 20-mm automatic cannons. The J29F pictured carries Sidewinder missiles.

In the context of Swedish Air Force history, 1945 may be regarded as the 'year of the jet'. In that year, it was decided to abandon the J27 project (an aircraft based on the 2,200-hp Rolls-Royce Griffon engine) and Flygmotor's development work on the 24-cylinder 2,500-hp Mx piston engine.

Despite some grounds for optimism —

Sweden was considered to hold something of a lead in the fields of turbines, combustion chambers, compressors and high-temperature materials — the Air Force Matériel Administration was not of the opinion that a jet engine suitable for powering a new fighter could be developed before 1952–53.

However, the Administration had clearly

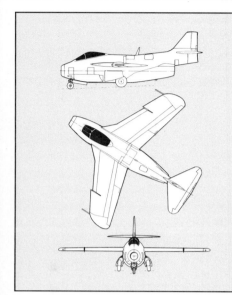

Saab 29 'Tunnan'

Interceptor, strike and reconnaissance aircraft

Versions	J29A, J/A29B, S29C, J29D, J29F		
Engine type/thrust	29A,B,C,E	*RM2 Svenska Flygmotor/De Havilland Ghost 50/2270 kgf (5004 lbf)*	
	29F	*RM2B Svenska Flygmotor/De Havilland Ghost 50 with afterburner/2800 kgf (6173 lbf)*	

	29A	**29B,C,E**	**29F**
Span, m (ft)	*11.00 (36'10¼")*	*11.00 (36'10¼")*	*11.00 (36'10¼")*
Length, m (ft)	*10.23 (33'6¾")*	*10.23 (33'6¾")*	*10.23 (33'6¾")*
Take-off weight, kg	*7530−8375*	*7530−8375*	*7530−8375*
(lb)	*(16600−18463)*	*(16600−18463)*	*(16600−18463)*
Maximum/cruising speed, km/h	*1035/800*	*1035/800*	*1060/800*
(mph)	*(643/497)*	*(643/497)*	*(659/497)*
Landing speed, km/h (mph)	*220 (137)*	*220 (137)*	*220 (137)*
Range, km (miles)	*1200 (750)*	*1500 (930)*	*1100 (680)*
Max. altitude, m (ft)	*13700 (44950)*	*13700 (44950)*	*15500 (50850)*

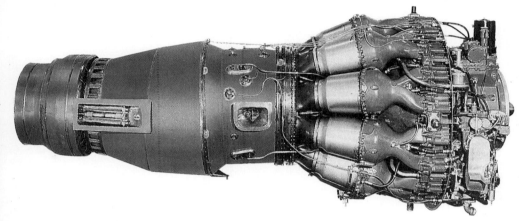

The RM2 engines installed in the 646 'Tunnans' logged a total of 714,256 flying hours.

reckoned without the combination of Saab and Flygmotor − and a prototype of the J29, popularly known as 'Tunnan' (or the 'Flying Barrel'), made its maiden flight on 1 September 1948.

In the interim, the Air Force purchased De Havilland Vampires powered by the Goblin engine, which was built under license by Flygmotor and had proved ideal for converting the J21 to jet propulsion.

The minor miracle of achieving the first test flight at this early stage was a tribute to the combined experience of the two companies. De Havilland had entrusted Flygmotor with the production of its more powerful Ghost engine, while Saab had already proved its ability to build airframes.

In somewhat exaggerated terms, the overall design problem might have been defined as one of building a top-class aircraft around a specific engine with a nose intake.

The nickname was coined by Chief Design-er Lars Brising on seeing the first conceptual sketches of the design in October 1945.

The pilot was perched on top of the air intake like a rider on a horse, the structure being completed by a fuselage boom and a tail section. The swept wings were a novel feature on a European fighter. On a visit to Switzerland, one of Saab's engineers had acquired copies of several Luftwaffe research reports on delta-wing design, which the Allies had seized after the war. American intelligence was obviously unfamiliar with technical German (a situation reminiscent of the B17 project) and the documents had aroused little interest − except in Sweden. The reports dealt with a series of wind-tunnel tests showing that swept wings had the effect of reducing drag dramatically as the aircraft approached the sound barrier. Subject to certain modifications based on safety considerations, the wings on the 'Barrel' were designed with a 25° sweep.

Lars Brising, project leader of the 'Tunnan' team. A British test pilot said of his creation: "It was love at first sight. On the ground, an ugly duckling − in the air, a swift".

Equipped with a scaled-down version of the 29 wing, a Saab 91A Safir was used to test the stability of the design, the swept-wing aerodynamics and the location of the slots and flaps.

The J29 played a major role in the development of Sweden's modern air defense system, based on an expanded network of bases and combat operation centers.

Production proceeded without delay once the design was completed (preparations having been initiated even before the inaugural flight in 1948) and the first production aircraft were delivered to F13 Wing in Norrköping in May 1951.

The J29B prototype was flown for the first time on 11 March 1953. Fitted with extra fuel tanks and armed with napalm bombs and rockets, the new version was designed for an attack role. In 1954, the plane set a world speed record, covering a 500-kilometer circuit (311 miles) at an average speed of 977 km/h (607 mph).

The photo-reconnaissance version (J29C) was something of a one-man job. While the first sketches were being prepared at the request of the Matériel Administration, Air Commodore Beckhammar, Chief of Reconnaissance Wing F3, contacted Saab with the following message: ''I'm not particularly happy with Staff's proposals. I'll bring down a truck with all the gear I think you should fit''.

An hour later, the designers were attacking

a wooden mock-up of the J29 with an ax — and eventually succeeded in squeezing in most of the equipment! The end product — known as the S29C — was built to more or less the same specifications as this first 'modified' version, becoming, in its day, the best-equipped reconnaissance plane in the world. The J29C also broke the world speed record over a 1,000-kilometer circuit (621 miles), raising the previous figure of 822 km/h (511 mph) to 906 km/h (563 mph).

The J29F (the last of the series) was equipped with a Swedish-designed afterburner which greatly boosted the engine thrust. The plane was also armed with two heat-seeking Sidewinder missiles.

In the words of one commentator: "The J29 became synonymous with the striking efficiency and power of the Royal Swedish Air Force. At the height of the aircraft's fame, the RSAF was fourth in size among the world's air forces, and the 'Flying Barrel' was a major weapon in the defense of the Nation's neutrality".

The J29 attracted interest in aviation circles throughout the world and might have become a major Swedish export. The Austrian Air Force bought a total of 30 used planes, while negotiations were also pursued with Chile and Israel without, however, reaching fruition.

Apart from the Swedish planes attached to Finland's F19 Squadron in 1940, the 'Barrel' was the only Swedish-built military aircraft ever to have taken part in action. This occurred during the Congo crisis in 1961 when five J29Bs operating under the UN flag destroyed the Katangan Air Force.

In all, Saab produced 661 of the series (the largest to date), the last of the planes being delivered in May 1956.

The 'Flying Barrel' flew for the last time on 29 August 1976 when "giddy with joy as in its days of glory, it tumbled through the skies over Malmslätt Airfield, heralding the end of an epoch with few parallels in the world of aviation". By then, the plane had completed 28 years of service.

Production of the 'Tunnan' called for 13,000 special tools, in addition to 150 large-scale assembly jigs. The standards of accuracy were such that the production of special measuring tools was also required.

The 1,000th Saab 92 was completed in late Fall 1950. In all, 1,246 cars were built during the year.

1950 — UNDER NEW MANAGEMENT

In May, Ragnar Wahrgren resigned his position as President of Saab and was succeeded by Tryggve Holm, a mining engineer by profession.

Available plant capacity was now completely booked by orders from the Matériel Administration under the terms of the current agreement (mainly for the new J29 jet plane) and production of the Scandia airliner, making it necessary to consider expansion. Although the shortage of labor had been solved by hiring workers from a number of European countries, plant expansion would cost at least SKr4million ($0.8 million). An additional factory was purchased in Jönköping for "the manufacture of assemblies and special equipment", to quote the cautious statement in the minutes.

Car manufacture was now under way, however slowly. Running initially at four cars per day, production for the year totaled 246. At least one production problem had been rationalized — all of the cars were green. The Defense Forces had purchased large quantities of a green cellulose paint for camouflage purposes. However, since the color proved to be a poor match for the green of the Swedish forests (the 'concealed' equipment actually being easier to locate), the paint was sold off to Saab, who used it on its cars for quite some time. In fact, it was to be three years before the car became available in another finish!

1951 — COLD WAR

Military orders again increased in volume as the Cold War cast its shadow and the Korean War broke out. Research and development work on new aircraft had produced the J29 'Flying Barrel', which was to become one of the best planes ever built by Saab. Improvements were also made to the Safir, which was bought by the Air Force for use as a trainer. As plant capacity became stretched to breaking point, some civil aircraft production was sub-contracted, the Safir and Scandia both being built in the Netherlands.

The Company's workforce was as hard pressed as its production facilities. Skilled workers were in short supply and major efforts were made to recruit abroad. The number of hourly-paid employees increased by 17% since the previous year.

Importing workers was merely a first step; major efforts were then required to ensure their social integration. Since the authorities were parsimonious with their building quotas, Saab was obliged to exert considerable pressure to obtain the requisite planning permission for housing. Language teachers and trade instructors were also needed.

Several works council members raised the matter of the trustworthiness — and productivity — of the foreign workers. (The council had just mounted a major campaign against "industrial espionage and sabotage by rumor-mongering", pointing out that such activities had, in fact, occurred.) In reply, the Chairman stated that all workers were carefully screened and that "the cost of hiring foreign workers should not greatly exceed that of retraining Swedish operatives".

The price of the car was increased to SKr 8,800 ($1,800) as a result of new tax provisions. Meanwhile, Gunnar Philipson, director of Philipsons Automobil AB, was pointing out that "to make the car a more attractive product, it should be modified by the provision of a trunk lid and a larger rear window and, if possible,

*Tryggve Holm
President of Svenska Aeroplan
AB, 1950—1967*

by increasing the headroom in the rear to make the back-seat accommodation more comfortable''. In compliance with these wishes, it was decided that a new version of the car would be introduced in 1952.

Otherwise, Saab owners appeared to be an extremely patient breed. One book about the marque included this passage: ''Saab drivers considered themselves a select brotherhood, treating the comments of other, less appreciative drivers on its spluttering, smoking and poor rearward visibility with patient forbearance''.

1952 – STABILITY

The new model (the 92B) was introduced in the Fall, completely absorbing whatever production capacity was not being used for aircraft manufacture, and it was obvious that further expansion would be required if the demand for the car increased. Exports had not been established on a regular basis.

The excellent performance of Saab cars in the competitive arena (pages 42–43) was obviously one of the main contributory factors to the success of the sales drive. A journalist recalls: ''When Greta Molander won the Monte Carlo Rally in a 92, she was asked 'Have you got an atomic bomb in the car?' Greta knew better – she had achieved her impressive speeds of 115–120 km/h (71–75.5 mph) thanks to larger carburetors and ignition coils – not atomic bombs''.

Another excellent sales argument was provided by the system of spare parts depots established in Europe for the benefit of touring motorists. Facilities had already been established in Brussels and Amsterdam, while others were planned for Paris, the Mediterranean coast and Hamburg.

However, some problems persisted; the shortage of sheet steel was creating acute difficulties. President Tryggve Holm commented ''The situation is particularly annoying when one considers that the Americans could roll Saab's entire annual requirement of 1,600 tonnes in a couple of hours''.

The wind tunnel for testing aircraft aerodynamics. Supersonic air flows were provided by four Goblin engines (the same type as the J21R powerplant).

Rally history

Greta Molander and Rolf Mellde achieved some of Saab's earliest successes in competition. The picture shows the two at the start of the 1950 Monte Carlo Rally.

Most of Saab's rally cars were red. Not until 1976 did they become as colorful as this one driven by Per Eklund and Björn Cederberg in the Thousand Lakes Rally in Finland.

Driving a Saab 92, K.G. Svedberg won the Circuit of Östergötland Endurance Rally the very month (December 1949) the model entered series production. A bare month later, two Saabs went to the start of the Monte Carlo Rally — the most prestigious competition of its type. Driven by Svedberg/Rolf Mellde and Greta Molander/Margareta von Essen, the cars (bearing chassis numbers 7 and 8) finished in 69th and 55th places respectively.

Rally activities subsequently acquired a momentum of their own. Rallying was the responsibility of the Test Department which modified the production models when the drivers reported weaknesses in the design. Ultimately, the standard models were so durably built that it was unnecessary to reinforce the bodies for competition purposes, although the engines used in the rally models were three times as powerful as those in the production versions.

It was not long before the Saab engines were uprated to outputs comparable to those of their competitors, added to which the Saab drivers discovered a driving technique which was later to become standard among rally drivers. This involved keeping the accelerator pressed to the floor, while using the left foot for braking as and when required, enabling a consistently high engine speed to be maintained and allowing the driver to corner by throwing the rear end in the 'right' direction. Gear changing was simplified by the freewheel, making it unnecessary to remove the left foot from the brake to declutch. Only a robust and well-designed car could have withstood treatment of this type.

The 3-cylinder Saab 93 and its successor, the 96, were exactly the cars which the rally drivers needed to hold their own in competition, and the triumphs which they achieved opened up many new markets for the make. Second place in the 13,000 km (8,100 miles) Tour d'Europa Rally, followed by victory in the inaugural Great American Mountain Rally in 1956, were the best possible advertisements which the new model could have received.

Built purely as a competition model, the first Sonett competed in an exhibition race in 1957. All concern for the driver and mechanic had been unceremoniously dispensed with — speed alone being the objective. However, the car never received a chance on the rally scene. In 1958, the competition rules were altered to permit the entry of 'Special Standard' models which, in Saab's case, meant the 93 with a Sonett engine and a chassis stripped of all superfluous weight.

Being easy to modify, the original 38-hp, 2-cycle engine was soon available in 50-hp and 60-hp versions. Furthermore, Saab had by now engaged a test driver named Erik Carlsson who was destined to become a legend.

Driving Saabs, Carlsson won the British RAC Rally three times running from 1961 to 1963, in addition to two Monte Carlo Rally triumphs in 1962 and 1963 and victories in a series of track races.

In keeping with the optimistic belief of the time that "everything is possible given enthusiasm and enough baling wire'', a Saab 93B was even entered in the major Le Mans 24-hour race in 1959. Stripped of nearly all fittings and equipped with a 98-liter fuel tank, the car completed 232 laps, coming 12th of the 13 finishers from the original field of 55. In the words of the race commentator, it was ''A remarkable achievement!''

Rallying quickly outstripped the resources of the Test Department and a special Rally Department was established in the early 1960s.

The 2-cycle unit, now with a cubic capacity of 841 cm³, had been successively uprated to 86.5 hp, an output at which it became extremely difficult to drive. The solution was to equip the 96 with a V4 engine.

The rally specialists modified the unit to the limit, resulting in victory for Saab in the inaugural Riihimäki Rally with Åke 'the Brewer' Andersson behind the wheel.

However, activities were concentrated mainly in Sweden where an impressive series of national championship victories was recorded, although the V4 also won the RAC Rally on two occasions.

At a juncture when competition from the light, special models built by other makers was becoming difficult for Saab, the Rally Department produced the next trump card from its secret workshop. The new model — a Saab 99 with twin overhead camshafts and 220 hp under the bonnet — swept to victory in its very first rally, the Boucles de Spa European Championship event held in Belgium.

Then came the Saab 99 Turbo. All of 1978 was devoted to tuning this model which was

destined to become the Company's last official rally car. Although its RAC Rally debut ended in disappointment when the driveshafts sheared, the 99 became the first turbocharged car to win a World Championship event (the 1979 Swedish Rally) — a clear demonstration of the basic excellence of the model.

Later that year, Company management very reluctantly decided to withdraw officially from rallying. The international rules had been altered to such an extent that only cars built to highly specialized specifications — versions with little in common with Saab's standard models — stood a chance of victory.

The fastest of Saab's rally cars, the Saab 99 Turbo became the first-ever turbocharged model to win a world championship event. However, based as it was on a standard model, the car was unable to match the 'specials' permitted under the new rules.

Erik 'On-the-Roof' Carlsson, a great rally driver in a great little car — a combination admired throughout the world for its skill and fighting spirit.

Saab 32 Lansen

The Saab 32 was an impressive high-technology aircraft. Hydraulics were used extensively in the design. The operation of one hydraulic component — the windscreen wiper — required no less than 8 horsepower!

Arthur Bråsjö, leader of the Lansen project, subsequently became Production Director.

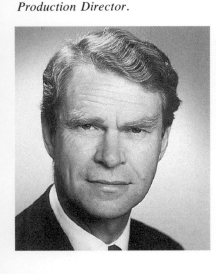

Events moved swiftly in the air-defense sector, and discussions regarding a successor to the 18B were under way even as the first of these aircraft were being delivered in the Fall of 1946. The shape of the next generation was already discernible from the preliminary design sketches; in line with American trends, the first proposal was based on a canard foreplane configuration (in which the tailplane is effectively located ahead of the wings) — a design which foreshadowed that of the Viggen several years later.

On 20 December 1948, Saab received the go-ahead to proceed with the first phase of development — the design and the construction of a mock-up of a conventional single-engined aircraft designated the 1150 or Aircraft 32. The time was obviously not ripe for a precursor of the Viggen.

The design work was characterized by a completely new approach in which the structure was designed by mathematical analysis rather than the familiar body-plan method. In the new system, the engineers developed a series of equations to produce coordinates which, when tabulated, yielded the appropriate parameters for each successive stage of the design.

Following the maiden flight of the first prototype on 3 November 1952, the test pilot reported: "The plane seems to be promising in all respects... The 32 will become a favorite with fliers...."

On 25 October 1953, the 32A became the first Swedish-built airplane to break the sound barrier.

The first production-line 32As were delivered to F17 Wing at Kallinge in December 1955, replacing the T18B.

The first prototype of the 32B — an all-weather interceptor equipped with a more powerful engine, heavier armaments, navigational and homing radar, a sophisticated fire-control system and an autopilot designed by Saab — flew for the first time on 7 January 1957. Known unofficially as the 'Lansen Sport', the plane was the Saab systems engineers' first step into the electronic age.

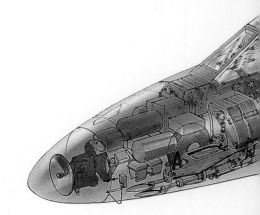

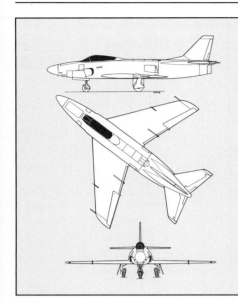

Saab 32 Lansen

Interceptor, strike, and reconnaissance aircraft

Versions	*A32A, J32B, S32C*
Engine type/thrust	*32A/C* *RM5A Svenska Flygmotor/Rolls-Royce Avon Mk21/3459–4695 kgf (7626–10351 lbf)*
	32B/D/E *RM6A Rolls-Royce Avon Mk47A/4790–6660 kgf (10560–14683 lbf)*

	32A/C	32B/D/E
Span, m (ft)	*13.00 (42'7¾")*	*13.00 (42'7¾")*
Length, m (ft)	*14.94 (49'0¼")*	*14.94 (49'0¼")*
Take-off weight, kg (lb)	*13600 (29982)*	*13500 (29762)*
Maximum/cruising speed, Mach	*0.91/0.8*	*0.93/0.8*
Landing speed, km/h (mph)	*210 (131)*	*250 (155)*
Range, km (miles)	*1850 (1150)*	*2000 (1240)*
Max. altitude, m (ft)	*15000 (49210)*	*16000 (52490)*

The next version – the 32C – was a reconnaissance aircraft equipped with five separate cameras. The plane made its inaugural flight on 26 March 1957.

A total of 447 Lansens of all types was produced, the last being retired from active service in 1973.

However, a number of modified 32Bs, known as 32Ds and 32Es, supplied to the Air Force Target Division, are expected to continue in service until into the next century.

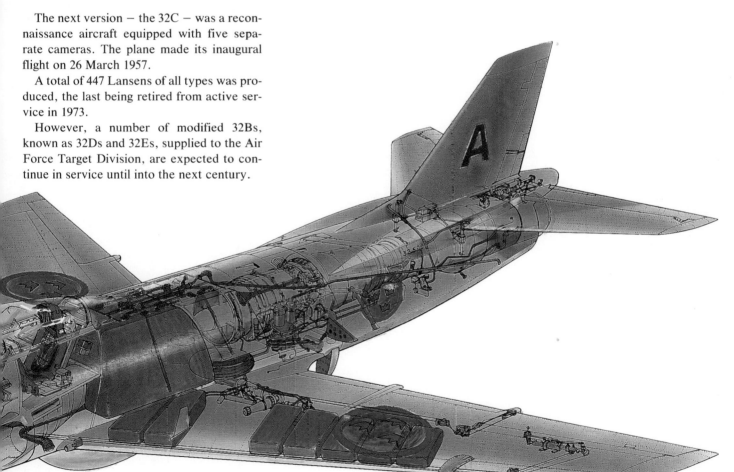

King Gustaf Adolf VI signing a J32 during his visit to the Linköping plant in 1953.

1953 – THE BIG BANG

"Company President Tryggve Holm informed the meeting that the Lansen had, just a short while previously, broken the sound barrier in the course of a test flight, adding that this was a matter for considerable satisfaction since the plane was not designed for such speeds" – a quotation from the minutes of the particular Board meeting.

The first prototype of the A32 Lansen had already flown the previous year and the aircraft which achieved this latest feat (in a dive and under "complete control") was one of three test planes. A correspondent to the Saab house magazine noted: "The event has made Sweden the fifth nation in the world to reach this milestone". And although its decision was not directly related to this remarkable performance, the Swedish Air Force ordered the new aircraft in numbers.

In view of the increasingly significant role which electronics were clearly destined to play in the control of aircraft and on-board systems, Company management decided to undertake the design and production of electronic products.

A new debutant made its appearance at the 25th International Motor Show in Geneva. Small and green, the exhibit attracted considerable attention. The car was, of course, the Saab 92, which the Company decided to show as a product capable of holding its own in export markets.

Another major step into the world abroad was taken with the conclusion of an agreement with a Brazilian company to build cars under license in São Paulo. However, new currency and import restrictions caused the abandonment of the agreement.

The scale of manufacturing operations was now such that existing facilities were inadequate and comprehensive reorganization was called for. A vacant washing-machine factory then for sale in Gothenburg appeared to be suitable as premises for manufacturing 15,000 engines annually, making room for an annual production of 5,800 to 6,000 bodies at Trollhättan. Transferring all aircraft production to Linköping at a later stage would enable this figure to be increased to 10,000.

A proposal to proceed with the above plan was approved by the Board.

1954 – WORLD'S FASTEST BARREL

The J29 broke a world record on 6 May when, with Captain Anders Westerlund from Uppland Wing at the controls, the aircraft achieved an average speed of 977 km/h (607 mph) over a 500-km (311 miles) circuit. The plane was a standard J29 which had not been modified in any way. The previous record of 950 km/h (590 mph) had been held by a US F86 Sabre.

Since modern combat aircraft were increasingly being designed as integral components of total defense systems – a development which, in itself, was nothing novel to Saab engineers – the Board decided to establish a special 50-man department specializing in operations analysis and systems technology.

As part of the relocation program carried out in 1953, production of the Safir was returned from the Netherlands to Linköping.

Competition in the car sector – particularly from Germany and France – was becoming stiffer and, despite increases in both sales and production over the previous year, the stockpile of finished cars was alarmingly high.

Not content with breaking speed records, Saab also exceeded all previous

The sound barrier

The sound barrier is the popular term used to describe the speed of an aircraft as it reaches the speed of sound. At an air temperature of 15°C, this is equivalent to 1,224 km/h (761 mph) at sea level, or 1,062 km/h (660 mph) at an altitude of 11,000 meters (36,100 ft).

The speed of the plane in relation to the speed of sound in the surrounding air is measured in terms of Mach number. Mach 1 represents the sound barrier.

Drag increases as the aircraft approaches Mach 1, falling again as the plane passes through the sound barrier. This phenomenon is due to the fact that the shock wave created as the aircraft approaches sonic speed is transferred to a point behind the plane.

levels of capital investment, with the commitment of more than SKr 20 million ($4 million) to the provision of new premises and machinery, with the aim of achieving an annual production of 10,000 cars. The decision may have appeared paradoxical, given the number of cars already stockpiled; however, the facilities were intended for the production of the new Saab 93, which was introduced in December 1955.

A brief extract from the Annual Report is worthy of quotation: "A Saab electronic computer is being developed in collaboration with the Swedish Board for Computing Machinery". Nobody could have suspected that this project was to lay the foundation for Datasaab, which was later to become one of the Company's most important divisions.

Captain Anders Westerlund getting into the world-record breaking J29.

1955 – A LARGE ORDER

The 'Flying Barrel' achieved another world speed record in March – in this case, for aircraft flying a 1,000-km (621 miles) circuit in pairs. Flying the S29C reconnaissance version, Captain Hans Neij and Second Lieutenant Birger Erikson achieved an average speed of 900.6 km/h (559.6 mph), breaking the existing record of 822 km/h (510.8 mph) set in 1950 by a Gloster Meteor Mk 8.

Production of the A32 Lansen proceeded according to plan, the Air Force taking delivery of the first production models during the year.

Development work on a supersonic aircraft had now progressed to the stage of the first prototype test flight – that of the 35 Draken. Since the ever-increasing complexity and higher speed of modern aircraft meant that flying experience alone was no longer sufficient training for a test pilot, Saab decided to establish a special pilot training course in subjects such as aerodynamics, mathematics, instrumentation, engine technology, aeronautic medicine and report writing.

The new car model, Saab 93, was shown for the first time in December. In this case also, Philipsons contracted to purchase the entire output at SKr 6,000 ($1,200) per car. The price (which was cut to the bone) was SKr 300 ($60) higher than anticipated. In its profit forecast for the coming year, Saab expected to break even in car production.

The men behind the J35 Draken. From left: Bengt Olow, Test Pilot; Erik Bratt, Project Leader; Tryggve Holm, President; Lars Brising, Technical Director, Aeronautics Department; Tord Lidmalm, Design Office Manager; Hans Eric Löfkvist, Head of Aerodynamics Department and Kurt Lalander, Head of Test Department.

Although the lines of the Saab 93 were similar to those of the 92, many features of the new model were radically different. For example, the front section was completely restyled and the engine was a new, more powerful unit.

Launched on 1 December 1955, the Saab 93 differed from its predecessor, the 92, in several major respects. The engine was a long-itudinally-mounted 3-cylinder unit which delivered a higher output despite its smaller displacement. The earlier torsion bars were replaced by coil springs and the car was fitted with tubeless tires. In effect, the model was a completely new car in terms of appearance as well as technical features. The number of 93s produced by the end of the year was 457.

The Company's marketing experts had set their sights on the US market even at the project stage, and a couple of notable rally successes paved the way for the model's introduction. The most outstanding of these was achieved when the car made its US debut in the Great American Mountain Rally in 1956. Saab entered three cars in the event and made a clean sweep of the overall, class and team awards (see page 42).

The sales organization consisted of a sub-

The engine in the 93 was a 33-hp, 748-cm³, 3-cylinder unit mounted longitudinally. Coil springs were another innovation.

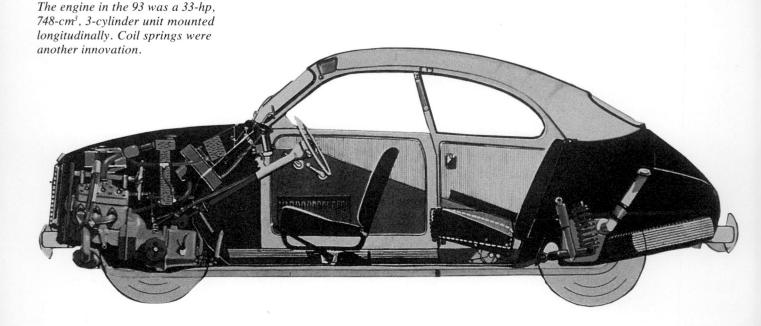

sidiary, Saab Motors Inc., and a sales office in New York. In the first year of operations (1957), 1,410 cars, representing 14% of total production, were sold in the USA.

To meet the demand, substantial capital was invested in the Trollhättan plant and the first-phase production target of 10,000 cars annually was also achieved in the first year. Output reached 17,836 units in 1959. Of total production up to and including that year, 12,000 cars were exported to the USA.

No major modifications were made during this entire period. The 1958 model, known as the 93B, was the first to boast a significant number of new features, mainly to enhance safety and performance, while a further-improved version emerged from the Saab Sonett experiment. Designated the GT750, this was designed specifically for the American market and was aimed at buyers interested in a sportier and more luxurious model than the standard 93. The new version was equipped with a sports steering wheel, rev counter and speed pilot. However, the most important refinement lay in the engine which was modified to deliver an additional 12 hp. Of the 600 GT750s manufactured, 546 were sold in the USA.

Another experimental version of the 93 was the 'Monster' − a model which was stripped of all superfluous components and equipped with 1.5 liters of power in the form of two 748-cm³ engines. The car was built for the purpose of beating the world speed rec-

Saab 93, 1956−1960

Length/width/height: 401/157/147 cm (158/62/58 in)
Three-cylinder, 2-cycle, 748-cm³, 33-hp,
longitudinally mounted engine
Three-speed transmission with freewheel
and column-mounted gearshift
Independent suspension, coil springs front
and rear
Drum brakes all round with parking brake
acting on rear wheels
Top speed: approx. 120 km/h (75 mph)

2-door Sedan

ord for models of this cubic capacity. Although the attempt as such was successful (the car reaching 198 km/h, or 123 mph), the organizers had forgotten to appoint official test scrutineers, and since the run was completed in one direction only, the speed could not be recognized as a record. One last attempt ended in a transmission failure.

The lone 'Monster' was built to make an attempt on a world speed record. The twin-engined experimental car is now on display in the Saab Museum at Trollhättan, which is open to all visitors.

Saab cars were available with the option of a 'Saxomat' clutch in the days before automatic transmission. Since the unit was operated by a switch on the gearshift lever, only brake and gas pedals were required. The lever seen in the upper right-hand corner of the picture was for engaging and disengaging the freewheel.

The highway was practically abandoned as a test track as early as in the 50s, although road testing is still an important element in test programs. Since the cars cannot be subjected to sufficiently high stresses on the road, special facilities, complete with a test track and vibration test rig, were built at Trollhättan.

49

Combat aircraft systems and avionics

Aerial combat during the Second World War was not only a 'man-to-man' but often an 'eye-to-eye' affair, fought with aircraft designed to fly at about 500 km/h (310 mph).

Then came two technical breakthroughs that were to completely alter the tactics of aerial warfare and revolutionize the development of warplanes. The first was radar – the system of using radio waves to measure distance. Invented by engineers working for the Allies, and used initially by the Royal Air Force to alert its fighters to the approach of German bombers across the Channel, enabling them to climb to a suitable altitude from which to attack, the system was quickly adapted for installation in aircraft. This advance caused the German Luftwaffe considerable puzzlement. All of a sudden, British planes were mysteriously able to find their way through darkness and fog and to detect German aircraft at long range, even when they sought to hide in the clouds.

The second breakthrough was the development of a new type of engine based on the reaction principle. The jet engine, as it became known, dramatically increased aircraft speeds and climbing performances, greatly expanding their scope of operation.

The installation of on-board radar paved the way towards the development of modern 'system' aircraft. Until then, the effectiveness of an aircraft had been completely dependent on the skill of the pilot, who was forced to make tactical decisions on the basis of his own judgments, often under severe stress.

Radar provided pilots with the exact information needed to carry out combat maneuvers. Since then, aircraft have been equipped with increasingly faster and more responsive sensing and information-processing systems, to assist pilots in maximizing the effectiveness of their planes and fulfilling their missions. For example, aircraft can be 'locked' onto and guided automatically to a specific target.

Saab-Scania aircraft designs reflect the course of development. The first airplanes, from the B17 to the 'Tunnan' and Lansen, all represented milestones on the road to supersonic types, while the even greater effectiveness of the Draken and Viggen was attributable to advances in avionics – as will that of the Gripen. The increased miniaturization of electronic components has enabled modern aircraft to be equipped with the most complex and powerful systems.

The first electronic aids – radio and navigational systems – were installed in the 'Tunnan' and Lansen in the 50s. The work was carried out by the Swedish Air Force Matériel Administration, which purchased the equipment and installed it in the aircraft in its own central maintenance workshops.

The D and F versions of the Draken were equipped with a target-ranging system which employed radar to inform the pilot of the exact instant at which to fire his weapons. In the F type, the radar system is integrated with heat-seeking missiles designed to seek out, lock onto and destroy the target.

As the individual components of the systems became more and more complex, they were purchased by the Administration from several different suppliers. Coordination and matching with the aircraft systems was carried out by Saab-Scania, which was later assigned responsibility for the actual installation work.

The first electronic computers designed to perform technical calculations were built in the mid-50s. Based on digital technology, these machines were so huge that they filled complete offices. Saab and the Administration took what was unquestionably a daring decision in the late 50s when they decided to undertake the development of an on-board computer (or 'tactical calculator' as it was first known). The system was intended for use in the Viggen, making the strike version the first operational aircraft in the world to be equipped with this feature.

Earlier strike aircraft up to and including the Lansen required a navigator to assist the pilot – a necessity which was now eliminated. The Viggen was built in a range of versions, largely because the avionics were designed so specifically for the different roles and armament configurations of the aircraft.

The next stage of development was the installation of a series of computerized systems, including a master computer and electronic display equipment, in the interceptor version of the Viggen, together with other systems such as radar.

Although the Air Force was still sourcing most of the avionics components used in the aircraft, some were also being purchased through Saab-Scania. In time, the Company became the main systems contractor, with re-

sponsibility for the coordination (in both technical and scheduling terms) of development work and equipment deliveries by subcontractors. A central coordinating function, which was subsequently reorganized into a systems electronics department, was established at Saab-Scania to this end. Purpose-designed systems simulators were built for software development.

By the time planning of the Gripen was commenced, systems technology had advanced to the stage where the aircraft could be designed to provide defensive capability under all weather conditions, in all visibilities and at all altitudes. This will also permit deployment of the aircraft in interceptor, strike and reconnaissance roles.

The plane itself carries both the hardware and software required for the particular role, the pilot being provided with three CRTs supplying all the information required for the successful completion of his mission. The avionics system consists of about 30 computers.

Aircraft systems coordination is the re-

sponsibility of the IG JAS Group, which is building the complete aircraft on behalf of the Matériel Administration.

The difference between the flying aces of the First World War (who were even known to salute enemy pilots whom they had just shot down) and the pilots of today's complex war machines is enormous. The role of the modern pilot is more that of a decision-maker and monitor. Historical and technological developments have produced 'programmable' systems aircraft which undergo continuous improvement and modification to meet the challenge of a constantly changing risk scenario. As a result, the aircraft operated by the Royal Swedish Air Force are among the best in the world in terms of performance.

One of the few photographs ever taken in a modern combat control center due to security restrictions. All information relating to enemy aircraft movements or missile attacks are received here and relayed to the pilots.

Saab 35 Draken

The armament of the most recent version of the Draken 35F includes Rb28 Hughes Falcon homing missiles built under license by Saab-Scania.

Saab was given an unusually free hand in designing the J35, its brief being ''to design a fighter for the interception of bombers operating at Mach 0.9, at an altitude of 11,000 meters (36,000 feet). The plane shall be armed with two air-to-air missiles''. The only addition to these minimal specifications was contributed later by General Bengt Jacobson: ''Just build the best damn plane you can – so long as it has a tail!''

In the event, somewhat more detailed specifications emerged as design work progressed. The plane was to be an all-weather interceptor capable of supersonic flight and operation from small airfields. On the other hand, the 'tailplane' – essentially a stabilizer mounted on a strut behind the fin – was deemed to be 'unflyable' and never became more than a detail on a reject drawing.

Preliminary design work commenced in 1949 – despite the skepticism of some observers (including experts from the Royal Institute of Technology in Stockholm) who maintained that an aircraft capable of exceeding 750 km/h (466 mph) would never be built. In the event – rather like the famed bumblebee, which flits about busily, blissfully unaware that it cannot fly – the J35 eventually reached Mach 2.

Truth to tell, however, the Saab engineers did not possess a great deal of expertise in supersonic flight; neither had the way been shown abroad. ''We started with the cross-section of the plane – simply because we had to begin somewhere – figuring that drag would be reduced at supersonic speeds by making the sectional area as small as possible''. Mathematical analysis also indicated that a double-delta wing offered the best possible configuration for a supersonic plane. Practical tests were carried out using tethered models, and engineers were even seen flying paper planes through the offices in efforts to determine how the design would behave in practice.

In the end, the designers' uncertainty was such that it was decided to build a test aircraft to a scale of about 70% before producing an actual prototype.

The 'Mini-Draken' (otherwise the Saab 210) was completed on 21 January 1952, nine

Engineer Eric Bratt gives Test Pilot Bengt Olow his final instructions prior to the maiden flight of the Draken on 25 October 1955.

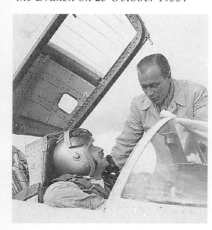

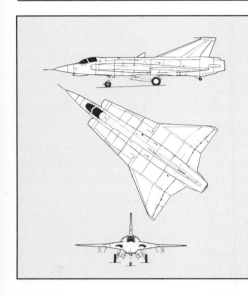

Saab 35 Draken

Interceptor, reconnaissance and training aircraft

Versions	35A, B, C, D, E & F		
Engine type/thrust	35A/B/C	RM6B Svenska Flygmotor/Rolls-Royce Avon 200/4750–6340 kgf (10472–13977 lbf)	
	35D/E/F	RM6C Svenska Flygmotor/Rolls-Royce Avon 300/5800–8000 kgf (12787–17637 lbf)	

	35A/C	35B	35D,E,F
Span, m (ft)	9.42 (30'10¾")	9.42 (30'10¾")	9.42 (30'10¾")
Length, m (ft)	15.2 (49'10½")	15.34 (50'4")	15.34 (50'4")
Take-off weight, kg (lb)	9000 (19841)	9000 (19841)	12500 (27557)
Maximum/cruising speed, Mach	1.5/0.9	1.5/0.9	2+/0.9
Landing speed, km/h (mph)	300 (186)	300 (186)	300 (186)
Range, km	1375–2750	1375–2750	1375–2750
(miles)	(850–1710)	(850–1710)	(850–1710)
Max. altitude, m	13000–15000	13000–15000	13000–15000
(ft)	(42650–49210)	(42650–49210)	(42650–49210)

months and SKr 1.7 million ($340,000) later. Following a successful test flight, the Swedish Air Force ordered three full-scale prototypes.

The first batch of final drawings was issued by the design team (which finally numbered 200) in 1953, and the plane began to take shape towards the end of 1954. The last Saab aircraft to be designed on the drawing board, the J35 finally made its first flight on 25 October 1955.

The original intention had been to use a Glan engine made by STAL in Finspång. In the event, however, the production of this unit was halted and a Rolls-Royce powerplant was chosen instead. "The Rolls people were fantastic to work with. We used something called the Rolls-Royce envelope. Everything inside this was engine, everything outside airplane. As well as that, the dimen-

The 'Mini-Draken' was described by a Linköping newspaper as "the pocket attraction which men, women and children alike flocked to see".

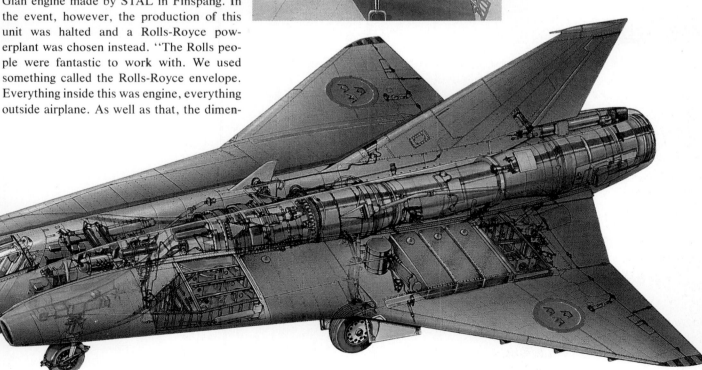

The 35 Draken has been defending the coasts of Sweden efficiently for close on 30 years — proof of the original sophistication of the design.

Test-firing a Saab RB05 strike missile from a 35 Draken.

sions were sacrosanct, which made the design of the airframe much easier".

The first prototype was not equipped with an afterburner. However, its successor, as the first to boast the feature, unintentionally broke the sound barrier (while climbing!) during its maiden flight. This performance was to make excellent sales material in marketing the plane abroad.

The 35B prototype was flown for the first time on 29 November 1959. The production model was equipped with sophisticated fire-control equipment for mounting collision-course offensives in coordination with the Swedish-built STRIL 60 air-defense system.

The training version (35C) — a modified 35A with the radar equipment and armament removed to make it a twin-seater — made its inaugural flight on 30 December 1959.

Equipped with the completely new Rolls-Royce RB Series 300 Avon engine with an afterburner, the 35D became the first Draken to reach Mach 2. The combined D/F prototype made its first flight on 27 December 1960.

The reconnaissance version, the 35E, had French-made OMERA cameras, and was test-flown on 27 June 1963.

According to the specifications, the Draken's landing distance was to be as short as the 'Flying Barrel's' (1,200 meters). This may be reduced even further using a brake chute, for example when landing at a highway base.

New flying kit was tested as part of the Draken test flight program. The photograph shows test pilot K.-E. Fernberg wearing an American-designed pressure suit with a fully sealed helmet − a forerunner of the modern spacesuit.

Following the next major modification, the plane was re-designated the 35F. This version was fitted with a computer-aided sight, improved radar equipment and two or four Falcon missiles in addition to conventional armament. With the integration of the 35F in STRIL 60, the Swedish air-defense system became the most efficient in the world.

In all, 644 Drakens were built, 52 being sold to the Danish Air Force. Finland, in addition to purchasing a number of Swedish-built 35Bs, also produced 12 of the aircraft at its own Valmet plant. The most recent contract for the aircraft was signed in 1985 when the Austrian Air Force purchased 24 Drakens reconditioned by Saab-Scania.

The Danish training version of the Draken. An extra drop tank is normally fitted underneath the fuselage to extend the combat endurance of the plane. However, the aircraft is also equipped with the usual number of hardpoints for use in tactical roles.

55

1956 – SUNDAY DRIVING BAN

Saab created a sensation at the Stockholm Motor Show with its experimental model, the Saab Sonett Super Sport. Equipped with a highly tuned Saab 93 engine, the car was built to test the power unit under more extreme conditions. In addition, since the designers were anxious to acquire more experience of plastics as body materials, the hood, rear section and doors were all of laminated fiberglass. Basically, the car was built on the same principles as an aircraft, using a box-section structure for mounting the chassis components.

Trouble in the Middle East, culminating in the Egyptian blockade of the Suez Canal, led to the world's first oil crisis. In Sweden, the result was a ban on Sunday driving by private motorists and the introduction of gasoline rationing. This had immediate repercussions on car sales; Volvo introduced a four-day week for its employees, although Saab announced 'business as usual'. Despite a fall-off in sales, Philipsons reported that stocks were nearly exhausted and needed to be replenished.

Saab was well-prepared. The previous year, its technicians had modified the Saab 92B to burn coal gas, using a refined version of the old Svedlund producer gas unit developed during the war. In its modified form, the 92 had a top speed of 70 km/h (43 mph). In this context, it is worth recording that Saab rose from ninth to fifth place in the sales statistics.

Rumors to the effect that Saab was about to establish a major division to produce what were then known as 'calculators' became persistent. Since substantial investment capital would be required for this purpose — Government monies could be used only for aircraft production — the stories caused considerable upheaval on the stock market.

Whether or not the rumors were true was of relatively little importance. Investors in the Company were certain to have been reassured by the Annual Report, which noted: "In 1956, both the military and civilian sectors achieved record performance in terms of invoiced sales and production value".

1957 – THE BRITISH PHOBIA

A British Government White Paper was the origin of what became known as 'the British phobia' in Swedish aviation circles. In the document, authoritative sources maintained that manned warplanes would soon become a thing of the past — systems and functions were becoming so complex and demanding that only robots would be capable of flying future aircraft. This view was shared by the Matériel Administration. In other words, the 35 would not have a successor, the plane being modified successively until such time as the robots took over.

The situation in the car sector also appeared to be critical. Concerned by the rapid growth of motoring, the authorities were widely rumored to be considering restrictions in the form of higher taxes, duties and similar measures.

The defense plan submitted by the Supreme Commander was the final straw. Even the most expensive alternatives were to involve substantial cuts in aircraft orders and redundancies of up to one thousand Saab employees.

However, Saab was not the only party which needed to look to its affairs. The finances of the Matériel Administration were in a mess, a commission appointed by Finance Minister Gunnar Sträng reporting a shortfall of SKr 180 million ($36 million) in its aircraft contracts. Both the Lansen and Draken had proved consid-

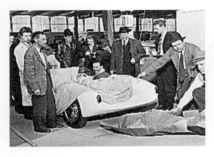

The Saab Sonett was the major sensation of the 1956 Stockholm Motor Show. Nobody outside the Company — not even Philipsons, Saab's Swedish agents — knew about the new car until the crate was opened.

The rate of output increased steadily, although some physically demanding tasks (such as fitting the wheels) could not be automated until the early 70s.

erably more expensive than originally estimated, due to higher labor costs and the cost of improving the technical specifications. For example, the Rolls-Royce engine used in the planes had undergone no less than 30,000 modifications since the start of production under license in Sweden.

The Government was finally obliged to request deferment of the payment. According to the records: "The Prime Minister inquired if Stockholms Enskilda Bank would be prepared to advance a loan sufficient to enable the RSAF Matériel Administration to meet its obligations. Mr. Wallenberg assented to the request, subject to the lodgment of promissory notes with the Bank, availing of the opportunity to seek information regarding the Government's long-term plans in the area".

The 50,000th Saab was a 1958 model 93.

At Saab, aircraft workers were trained as car assemblers, and SKr 30 million ($6 million) were invested in plant expansion with the aim of increasing the rate of production to one car every 5 minutes (compared with 11 minutes) and exporting 5,000 units annually by 1960. Referring to the problem of excise duties, management at Trollhättan commented: "It is important that we avoid panic. Instead, we must make skillful and enterprising use of the assets which we possess in the form of top-class technicians and workers".

1958 — A GOOD AND FAITHFUL SERVANT

After an association with Saab dating from its foundation, Torsten Nothin resigned as Chairman of the Board to be succeeded by Ambassador Erik Boheman. In his farewell speech, Marcus Wallenberg used the following terms to characterize his achievement of gathering the Swedish aircraft industry under a single umbrella: "Without Torsten Nothin's exceptional love of country, his clear appreciation of the importance of the task and his great authority, the matter could not have been resolved so expeditiously".

Some problems undoubtedly clouded the sky. Under the provisions of the defense plan approved by Parliament, considerable numbers of military orders were either deferred until later or had their delivery times extended, all of which created problems in the context of employment. However, prospects were more encouraging in the helicopter sector, Saab concluding a contract with Sud-Aviation of Paris to build and sell the Alouette II turbine-powered helicopter, 10 of which were ordered immediately by the Swedish Navy and Army.

The generally high level of interest in helicopters prompted the Company to introduce a range of services from the Norrköping plant. These included air taxi and ambulance flights serving the local archipelago, flying instruction, tourist excursions and other special assignments. In addition, single-engined and twin-engined passenger planes were to be supplied for air taxi services both at home and abroad.

The inaugural flight of the first production 35 Draken was scheduled for 15 February. The occasion was used to announce that a new version, expected to be capable of speeds in excess of Mach 2, was to be built shortly.

The demand for cars was substantial and production was increased accordingly, 324 cars (triple the 1956 output) leaving the assembly line each week. Workshop and warehouse capacities became inadequate to deal with this rapid expansion, and a 600 m² (6,500 ft²) marquee was erected in the grounds of the plant to store spare parts, alleviating the worst of the problems.

Erik Boheman
Chairman of Svenska Aeroplan
AB, 1958–1969

Saab 95

In May 1959, after ten years as an auto-maker, Saab expanded its range with the introduction of an estate model – the Saab 95. The first 95s were built from a curious mixture of components which were the best then available to the designers, and included items such as the 841-cm³ engine and 4-speed transmission developed for the 96 (which had not yet appeared), and the rear-hinged doors and instrument panel from the 93.

Production was also a remarkably flexible affair. Parts from stock unused at the end of the production year were utilized – a rational and economic approach which produced a highly versatile vehicle with a maximum payload of no less than 500 kg (1,100 lb). The interior space could be rearranged to accommodate 2, 5 or 7 passengers, a folding seat in the baggage compartment providing the sixth and seventh spaces. Since it faced the rear, this seat was usually a favorite with children, who enjoyed waving to cars behind.

Unfortunately, their view was not always the best, a deficiency which was rectified in 1961 with the introduction of the 'air wiper' – a device which kept the rear window free of the dirt which was swept up behind the car.

Otherwise, the 95 was modified in step with the 96. In keeping with the philosophy of always using the best components from other cars in the range, the last model (1978) was fitted with the front seats from the 99.

The total number of 95s produced was 110,527.

After its introduction in 1959, the Saab 95 underwent the same modifications as the 96. The only 'unique' feature was the 'air wiper' (right) which kept the rear window free of dirt by sweeping it with a flow of air.

All but the later 95s were equipped with an extra, backward-facing seat which was folded into the floor of the baggage compartment when not in use, making the car a 2, 5 or 7-seater as required.

Saab 96

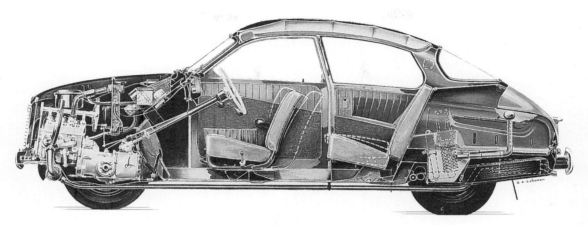

Saab unveiled its third model to the press in the fall of 1960. Known as the 96, the car remained a 'classic' Saab. Although the front was unchanged in appearance, the rear half of the car had been completely redesigned. The rear seat had been widened by 25 cm (10 in) and the trunk enlarged, while the rear lights were of a new design and the rear window was 117% larger. However, the re-modelled exterior concealed one of the main reasons for the immediate success of the car, annual production of which (including the 95) was increased to 50,000. This was the power train, consisting of an 841-cm³, 38-hp engine driving a 4-speed transmission, from 1962 on.

The first right-hand-drive Saab — a 96 exhibited in London — appeared the same year.

The 96 also enabled the Company to maintain its leading position in the field of rallying. The new competition rules which permitted the entry of modified production models had eliminated the Sonett, and Saab needed a

Saab 95, 1959—1978. Saab 96, 1960—1980

Length/width/height: 401/157/147 cm (158/62/58 in)
Three-cylinder, 2-cycle, 841-cm³, 38-hp, longitudinally mounted engine
Three-speed transmission with freewheel and column-mounted gearshift
Independent suspension, coil springs front and rear
Drum brakes all round with parking brake acting on rear wheels
Top speed: approx. 120 km/h (75 mph)

1964 model
Four-speed transmission

1965 model
Length: 416 cm (164 in)
40-hp engine

1967 model
V4, 4-cycle, 1,498-cm³, 65-hp, longitudinally mounted engine
Disc brakes at front
Top speed: approx. 145 km/h (90 mph)

1977 model
68-hp engine

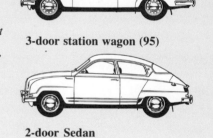

3-door station wagon (95)

2-door Sedan

In 1960, the Saab 96 body was restyled from the front doors back. Other modifications included a new instrument panel and a 38-hp engine. The front of the 1965 model (left) was modified and the car lengthened by 15 cm (6 in).

The complete range of 1966 models. From left: the Saab Monte Carlo, Saab 95 and Saab 96.

Initially, the 96 was fitted with an 841-cm³ engine—an enlarged version of the 2-cycle unit (seen above in the triple-carburetor version).

The 1967 Saab 96 was the first to be fitted with the new German-built, 4-cycle, 65-hp, V4 engine.

successor — a car which could readily be adapted to deliver a livelier performance than the standard version. The result was the Granturismo 750 (essentially a sportier 93B) which was introduced in 1958. From 1960 on, this was built on the new 96 chassis and was equipped with a 45-hp engine (compared with the 33-hp unit in the original 93B). Adopted as the standard engine, this was complemented by the new 4-speed transmission.

In 1962, the engine was fitted with triple carburetors and uprated to 52 hp. Equipped with a separate lubrication system, the car also ran on ordinary gasoline unmixed with oil. The model was known as the Saab Sport, except in the USA where it was sold as the Granturismo 850.

Only three years later in 1965, the maximum rating was increased to 55 hp and the following year, the car was renamed the Monte Carlo 850 to celebrate the legendary Erik Carlsson's victories in the car in that classic rally. The Monte Carlo model was discontinued in 1968.

In 1961, the 96 was fitted with two independent hydraulic brake circuits — a unique Saab design in which each of the circuits operated the brakes on one front wheel and the diagonally opposite rear wheel. This feature enabled the driver to maintain steering control while braking, even if one of the two circuits failed.

The sales graph, which had begun to take an alarming downswing, recovered strongly in 1967 when both the 95 and 96 were equipped with an overhead-valve, 4-cycle, V4 engine designed and built by Ford.

Production of the 96 ceased at the end of 1979, by which time a total of 547,000 had been built.

The Saab 96 achieved a series of major rally successes. The photograph shows Carl Orrenius on the first special stage of the Dacke-fejden Rally in 1967. The engine was modified to develop 105 hp.

The new car plant at Trollhättan was inaugurated in 1959, doubling annual production from 12,000 to 24,000 units. The plant was brought on stream at full output without losing production of a single car.

1959 – END OF AN EPOCH

"After cutting a blue and yellow ribbon in front of the row of cars on the final assembly line, County Governor Mats Lemne stepped back to allow a black Granturismo to pass, chauffeured by a driver in dazzling white overalls. As the GT moved off, a clamor of horns rose from all the other cars in the assembly shop". This description of the official opening of the new car plant at Trollhättan appeared in the Saab house magazine.

Although the capacity of the new plant was 30,000 to 40,000 cars per year, expansion to 60,000 within four years was being discussed even as the inauguration took place. The 1960 model of the new Saab 95 station wagon had now been added to the range. Although the bodies were produced in the aircraft plant presses at Linköping, painting and final assembly were carried out in Trollhättan. As part of the latest expansion, all aircraft production was transferred to Linköping, bringing an end to aircraft activities in Trollhättan.

In Norrköping, work on helicopter production proceeded rapidly and the first Swedish-built Alouette II was test-flown in May. Two machines had been built in less than a month! The first customer was the Swedish Navy.

Expansion of the range of cars called for corresponding development of the dealer organization. Philipsons, who had been sole agent for Saab until this time, were also marketing Mercedes-Benz, while one of their subsidiaries was selling DKWs in direct competition – a situation which prompted Gunnar Philipson to express doubts as to the "feasibility of expanding sales as we would wish". Immediate action was called for, the acquisition of an established sales organization being the ideal solution. At the very next Board meeting, the Chairman informed the gathering that "the Company has been invited to purchase all 3,000 shares in AB Nyköpings Automobilfabrik (ANA) at a unit price of SKr 5,000".

1960 – THE ELECTRONIC AGE

The Board accepted the offer to acquire ANA, which commenced to market Saab cars as from 1 September (Philipsons' sole rights being terminated on the same date). The new organization received a flying start in the form of the newly unveiled Saab 96 which was given a fantastic reception. As further incentives, all cars were sold with a 6-month warranty and buyers were offered a reduction of SKr200 ($40).

Motoring enthusiasts were excited by the appearance of another new creation in the form of an experimental racer built to Formula Junior rules (which specified that all essential engine and chassis components should be from a production model of one and the same type).

Exports to countries with left-hand traffic had now reached a volume which justified the production of right-hand-drive 96s from the beginning of the year on.

In conjunction with the design of the 32 Lansen, Saab took a definitive step into the electronic age with the establishment of a new division at Linköping, bringing all the Company's computer and electronics expertise together under a single roof. Apart from computer technology, the Division (known as Datasaab) was involved in all other industrial, medical and military applications in which advanced electronic equipment was used. Its first major product was the Saab D2, then the fastest calculator in Europe. Weighing 150 kg (331 lb), the unit was the first all-Swedish transistorized machine on the market and was capable of adding two 6-digit numbers 100,000 times per second.

For its own use, Saab installed the country's first computer designed exclusively for industrial applications. An 8-tonne giant, the machine was used for purposes such as payroll accounts, production planning, stock control and financial planning.

1961 – NEW FRAMEWORK AGREEMENT

During the year, the Company signed a new framework agreement governing its contracts with the RSAF Matériel Administration. Applicable until 1968, the new terms differed significantly from those of previous agreements, in that the Government's undertaking to order specific quantities of matériel had been superseded by a commitment to place long-term orders for individual projects. A further innovation was the introduction of a standard price whereby the two parties were to share the profits accruing from any rationalization measures introduced by Saab in the course of an individual contract. Saab was also appointed to build and sell Hughes Falcon missiles under license.

As a result of the agreement, Saab also began to increase its efforts to exploit the civil aircraft market, acquiring the Swedish agencies for the French Morane-Saulnier Rallye executive and leisure aircraft, and the Hughes 269A helicopter as steps in this direction.

From the Swedish Navy, Saab received an order to build a hitherto unproven amphibian known as a hovercraft – a vehicle designed to operate on land, ice and water.

Regardless of the whys and wherefores of automobile safety legislation, Saab introduced seat belts as standard equipment in its cars in 1961 – long before they became legally compulsory. (Another, later example was the introduction of headlamp wipers in 1971).

Demonstration of a Saab D2 computer in Stockholm. The machine signified Saab's breakthrough in computers. The D2 contained approximately 6,000 transistors and was capable of performing 40,000 multiplications per second.

Although the Saab Formula Junior was faster than its competitors, it was extremely difficult to handle. Built as an experimental model to test aspects such as the development potential of the engine, it completed two seasons of competition, driven by Erik Carlsson, Carl-Magnus Skogh, Gösta Karlsson and a number of others.

President Tryggve Holm turned the first sod for the new Linköping headquarters on 24 March 1961.

The car in the postwar era

The accumulation of chrome on the front and the size of American cars reached a peak in the early 50s. At this time, the popularity of the huge US models in Europe also began to decline.

Direct successors to the motorcycle, European bubble cars presented a stark contrast to their American cousins. Although not a great success, models like this Frua-designed Goggomobile coupé were at least attractive.

The first 'yankee battleship' appeared in Europe immediately after the Second World War. On the impoverished, war-torn Continent, the nickname given the futuristic American models could express either total admiration, envy or contempt, depending on national attitudes to the victorious USA. Although the advertisements for the 'new' cars referred to features such as the 'cascade grill', 'airplane wings' and so on, the models were actually prewar versions disguised with glittering chrome and advertised as new.

However, the real innovation appeared in 1948–49 in the form of the all-enveloping body. With its smooth sides and enclosed wheels, the new car possessed a basic shape which still survives today. No longer constructed from separate components such as a hood, fenders and cab, the new body was a harmonious, integrated whole.

Engines were also undergoing considerable development. The first high-compression type and the V8 engines introduced by Cadillac and Oldsmobile heralded the start of an era in which practically every American car after 1955 was equipped with a V8.

Automatic transmission was another American first introduced to the European market in the 50s.

In Europe, the second generation of popular cars had become a reality. (For reasons which are now part of history, the first 'people's car' had never achieved the success envisaged by the German Ministry of Propaganda during the war.) The plain people of Europe could now afford their own cars, and even if most of those on the market were small, underpowered and uncomfortable 'popular' models, the pride of their owners in realizing their dreams was unmistakable.

In Sweden, the Saab 92 and Volvo PV444 appeared on the scene. Conceived towards the end of the war, both cars achieved exceptional success as production gathered pace. By the end of the 50s, the Saab 92 and its successor, the 93, had climbed to 4th or 5th position in the Swedish sales statistics.

Although many Swedish motorists obviously bought a Saab for patriotic reasons, the car proved its quality by outlasting its competitors. Many of the popular cars launched during the 50s quickly passed into oblivion. Who, other than motoring historians, now remembers the Gutbrod, Champion, Lloyd or Goliath – not to mention Messerschmitt or BMW Isetta bubble cars?

In terms of engineering and style, European cars of the 50s reflected the American influence, featuring two-tone finishes, panoramic windshields and tail fins (which, however, the Saab designers were never tempted to add to their creations). Technically, however, the cars were of a strictly conventional design with a front-mounted engine driving the rear wheels.

The 60s witnessed the appearance of a small car which revolutionized accepted design thinking. The model in question was the BMC Mini, which boasted front-wheel drive and a transversely mounted engine. With its superb roadholding, the car represented a breakthrough for front-wheel drive – a development to which Saab's notable victories in the Monte Carlo Rally obviously contributed.

The arrival of the Renault 4 also upset a number of established concepts, more in

terms of general attitudes to the car as a material possession than in any technical sense. In an advertising campaign which achieved enormous success, the model was presented as an inverted status symbol; no longer the realization of a dream, the car was henceforth to be regarded as an everyday, utilitarian object.

It was logical, therefore, that the 60s should become known as the decade of safety. Passive safety features such as padded instrument panels and impact-absorbent steering columns presented no major design problems and soon became standard in all cars. In contrast, the area of active safety produced many interesting innovations such as disk brakes and dual-circuit brake systems (in which the Saab diagonally-split configuration was unique). Increasing numbers of makers also adopted front-wheel drive.

Developments during the 70s were naturally affected by the oil crisis. Cars became smaller, a phenomenon which was, perhaps, most apparent in the USA where the huge 'battleships' finally became a thing of the past and European cars were finding a flourishing market. The turbocharged engine — largely a Saab innovation — was beginning to replace the large gas-guzzling 6-cylinder and V8 units. Turbocharging endowed a 4-cylinder unit with equivalent performance

at greatly reduced fuel consumption, the additional power being used only when really needed, such as for faster and safer overtaking.

The 80s saw the advent of electronics. Fuel-injection control units were improved and new features such as Saab's APC (Automatic Performance Control) system were developed. APC is a feature which enables the engine to burn fuel of any octane number from 92 to 98 without the risk of damage, lowering the charge pressure if the engine begins to knock. Saab has also developed a revolutionary new ignition system known as Saab Direct Ignition (SDI), which greatly prolongs spark-plug life and ensures more reliable starting under all conditions.

Electronics have also been utilized to improve the climate in cars. Saab's Automatic Climate Control (ACC) system is designed to control the air conditioning in accordance with a preset temperature.

Saab has been in the forefront of development with remarkable frequency. As it is one of the smallest automakers in the world, the challenge to lead the field is probably all the greater.

The BMC 'Mini' popularized front-wheel drive in a great many countries. The model appeared 10 years after the first Saab.

The Saab 99 Combi Coupé was the first model which really combined the comfort of a sedan with the load capacity of a station wagon. A blend of elegance and practicability, the type was quickly copied by several makers.

67

1962 – FROM RED TO BLACK

Saab celebrated its 25th anniversary with all due pomp and circumstance. There was, indeed, reason for celebration; the loss of SKr 48,000 ($10,000) reported in the first year of operations had been transformed into a net profit of SKr 10 million ($2 million). Further cause for satisfaction was the fact that the price of the latest Saab car – now bigger, better equipped and safer than ever – had risen to only SKr 8,350 ($1,670) compared with SKr 7,900 ($1,580) ten years earlier. Had the increase followed the general trend in inflation, the price would have been SKr 10,900 ($2,180), excluding taxes and other surcharges.

Saab was now undergoing unprecedented expansion. As main contractor for System 37 (the new Air Force project) and manufacturer of 37,500 cars annually, the Company employed 11,500 people in its eight Swedish plants. Aircraft were being sold in eight countries and cars in forty, while a 3-year, SKr 120 million ($24 million) capital investment program was being implemented. These (together with the information that one-third of all Linköping residents had direct or indirect links with the Company) were the most significant figures in the optimistic press release issued to mark the anniversary.

However, full-scale 'war' was raging between Saab and the Ministry of Finance. With the impending computerization of population and taxation records in twenty Swedish counties, a Government committee had recommended the installation of IBM equipment. The Company demanded that the reasons for the decision (which had been kept secret) should be made public, claiming that "the D21 system proposed by Saab is superior". (Already being used by three major companies, the system was operating satisfactorily.)

Bishop Sven Danell commented: "In a humanitarian society, civil records must be based on a deep, many-faceted respect for the human being, dictated by a cultural heritage both Christian and democratic by tradition, and by the fundamental principle that the relationship between a citizen and the society in which he lives should not be reduced to the level of impersonality". The Bishop went on to urge "vigilance" in the face of the "computer revolution". The year being 1962, His Lordship was an unusually farsighted man.

The first D21 computer was installed by AB Skandinaviska Elverk, who used it for planning, forecasting and production scheduling.

1963 − DEATH OF A RUMOR

"We have as much intention of buying Saab as we have of entering the hornet's nest which is the small-car market!" With these words, Volvo President Gunnar Engellau quashed the persistent rumors of a merger between Volvo and Saab. In actual fact, the other party was more likely to be the buyer! Or, as the newspaper 'Aftonbladet' put it: "This Wallenberg wants a finger in every pie".

Although Saab's share of the Swedish car market had fallen from 12.8 to 11.7%, registrations had risen from 25,000 to 27,000. Hornet's nest or not, Company management had every reason for optimism when stating: "The level of orders is higher than twelve months ago − a satisfactory situation".

The prototype of the Saab 105 was ready for flight testing and 130 of the aircraft were on order. Commenting on the defense budget for the next four years, the Defense Committee reported: "Military and foreign policy developments in recent years do not suggest that the need for a strong defense can be relaxed".

Meanwhile, Saab's design engineers were working flat out on the top-secret Viggen project, leading the press to complain that "national security is quoted every time one attempts to ask a question about the Viggen". At the same time, an advertisement published by Saab in 'Aviation Week' almost caused a collective nervous breakdown in the Swedish secret service, since it included the most detailed illustration of the aircraft yet published.

Operating at a speed of 70 km/h (43 mph), the first hovercraft underwent initial testing − unfortunately without conspicuous success. The Navy refused to pay for the design in its existing form while, according to the Board's report: "A further SKr 200,000 ($40,000) will be required to develop the vehicle to the stage at which it will be more or less acceptable to the Navy".

The computer 'war' was resolved by adopting a typically Swedish compromise, Finance Minister Gunnar Sträng deciding that both IBM and Saab machines would be installed by the county councils on a trial basis.

Among other events, the Company made its 200,000th car, the new Linköping offices were officially opened, the first Falcon missiles were delivered − and IF Saab were promoted to the first division of the Swedish handball league.

Designed by Saab, Sweden's first hovercraft was tested in 1963. Known as the Saab 401, the vehicle was ordered by the Swedish Navy as part of its overall research program into the use of the type.

The Saabo was an attempt to produce a caravan designed specifically for the relatively small cars which Saab − and many of its competitors − were making in the early 60s. Despite its compact layout, it was of a highly advanced design.

Fifty years of aviation

Much-beloved of aviation enthusiasts, the old, faithful DC-3 is regarded as proof of the designer's cliché that good-looking aircraft fly well. Over 300 examples are still in military service around the world, while more are being restored as museum pieces by collectors.

Designated the PR Mk19, the Supermarine Spitfire was used in Sweden for reconnaissance duties.

The time scale of the title should, perhaps, be extended to 52 years to include the Douglas DC-3 — an aircraft which first took to the air in 1935 and which contributed more than any other to the development of worldwide commercial aviation as we know it today. By the time the USA entered the Second World War in 1941, 450 DC-3s had been delivered to airlines around the world. Although an impressive number in those days, this total was dwarfed during the War when more than 10,000 of the aircraft were built. Most airlines and air forces throughout the world have flown the DC-3; in fact, several hundred are in service to the present day.

Accommodating about 30 passengers, the plane had a maximum speed of 300 km/h (186 mph) and provided an excellent example of how modern construction techniques were beginning to take shape. The airframe consisted essentially of a shell made of light alloy — a design which quickly became predominant, lending itself to the creation of an efficient aerodynamic shape while minimizing weight. The construction was also ideally suited to mass production, even of sophisticated aircraft with individual lines. To reduce drag, the DC-3 was built as a monoplane with retractable landing gear — a configuration which rapidly made the earlier biplane obsolete. Furthermore, the aircraft could be parked outdoors, unlike the earlier fabric-covered timber or tubular-steel types, which were vulnerable to the weather.

The development of military aircraft followed the same pattern. Classic fighters such as the Hurricane and Spitfire in Britain and the Messerschmitt 109 in Germany were designed in the latter half of the 30s. Reliable engines were obviously a first priority and the piston engines of the day (normally air or liquid-cooled) delivered approximately 1,000 hp. This was far from adequate as payload and speed demands increased, and the designers quickly succeeded in doubling engine ratings. Delivered in 1938, the first mass-produced Spitfire had a top speed of 580 km/h (360 mph) and was powered by a 1,030-hp engine. In contrast, the last version of the plane (built in 1945) was equipped with a 2,350-hp unit and was capable of 730 km/h (454 mph).

In mechanical terms, the earliest piston engines were extremely complicated and far from providing a desirable standard of re-

liability. Furthermore, it was impossible to achieve a speed of more than 750 km/h (470 mph) using a combination of a piston engine and propeller — and the question was whether the ultimate aircraft speed had been reached.

The gas turbine supplied the answer. Using rotating elements rather than reciprocating pistons, the unit is mechanically simpler, lighter, more robust and — under certain conditions — less expensive for a given rating. With its introduction, aircraft speeds now began to approach 1,000 km/h (621 mph) and the optimists among the engineers began to dream of flying faster than sound.

For obvious reasons, the first gas turbine-powered aircraft (or jet planes as they were known) were developed for military purposes and were flying by the end of the Second World War. Although the early versions were noisy and extremely thirsty, these disadvantages were acceptable in the prevailing circumstances, the exceptional speed of the planes outweighing all other drawbacks.

The American experimental aircraft, the X-1, smashed the sound barrier on 14 October 1947. Although the plane was admittedly rocket-powered, the event confirmed that supersonic flight was possible and mass-produced aircraft were soon emulating the feat. Although initially achievable only in a dive, it was not long before speeds of Mach 2 became a reality.

Three generations of jet planes were designed by Saab-Scania during this period. Designated the J29, A32 and J35, these more than held their own in international competition, entering production at the same time as their foreign counterparts (and, in some cases, earlier). World speed records were broken on a couple of occasions by the J29.

Peace also gave civil air transport a major boost. Since the old DC-3 was unable to fly the longer routes, the next generation — in the form of the Douglas DC-4 and DC-6, and the Lockheed Constellation, all large four-engined propeller aircraft — were not long in appearing. These were used on long-haul services until the beginning of the 1960s.

A British jet airliner — the De Havilland Comet — entered commercial service in 1952, an event which seemed to offer conclusive evidence that the engine could also be used in civil aircraft. Flying times were to be halved, while passengers were to be spared the noise

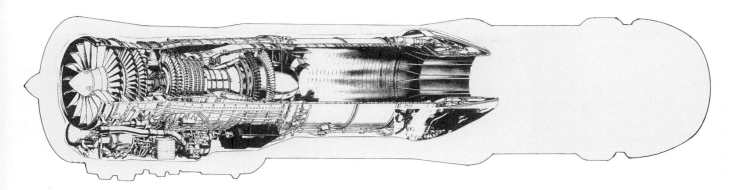

of the earlier piston engines and the standard of comfort was to be improved. The optimism was short-lived; three of the nine aircraft built crashed within a year and the plane was withdrawn from service. Metal fatigue was found to be the cause of failure and the entire episode proved to be a financial disaster for the makers. Nevertheless, producers of military aircraft around the world immediately applied the Comet experience to their own designs.

The gas turbine was also combined with the propeller to create an engine which became known as the turboprop. Although the propeller reduced the speed of the plane, the fuel consumption was less in comparison with the pure jet and the noise level was also lower. Several turboprop aircraft introduced in the 50s gave excellent service. Perhaps the best example of a successful design was the Fokker F27, which was produced for more than thirty years.

The development of jet airliners continued despite the Comet setback. Oil prices continued to fall throughout the 60s, and fuel economy took second place to speed. The relatively slow propeller aircraft used on the longer routes were replaced by the Boeing 707 in 1958, followed by the Douglas DC-8 in 1959 (when the French also entered the field with the Caravelle). The undoubted demand for the new standards of comfort and speed was demonstrated by the increase in traffic on the North Atlantic between 1958 and 1967, a period when the number of passengers rose from 1 million to 5 million annually.

The Caravelle was a major success, and jets were soon dominating the medium-haul sector also. Several efforts to build a supersonic airliner were made during the late 60s. However, the only plane of this type to enter commercial service was the British-French

Concorde – a project which was significant more in terms of national prestige than of economics.

The next generation consisted of wide-bodied aircraft (speed now being considered less important than improved fuel economy and comfort). The most famous example of this type is the Boeing 747 (known as the Jumbo), which can carry up to 550 passengers.

Commuter or regional traffic (in the form of short-haul feeder services) is a sector whose rapid development is of major importance to Saab-Scania. In this case, high-frequency services with smaller aircraft offer the best means of competition. Operating costs must be reduced to achieve viability – yet another goal which has been made possible by advances in engine technology. (A new generation of turboprops is now being used in this application.) Although speeds may be somewhat lower, the extra few minutes of flying time are far outweighed by the returns in the form of a 50% reduction in fuel consumption. The Saab SF340 (see page 120) is an excellent example of the new generation of small commuter turboprops.

It is interesting to note that military aircraft speeds have stabilized at about Mach 2, combat effectiveness being improved primarily by enhanced system performance. In other words, on-board avionics in the form of computers and sensors are becoming ever more sophisticated. In this sense, the Viggen is the precursor of a trend which will continue with the Gripen. The latter is also representative of another development – the use of modern technology to build an aircraft only half the size of its predecessor, although offering superior overall performance at lower cost.

A comparison between the sizes of the Viggen and Gripen engines. New technologies and materials have reduced the weight of the Gripen's powerplant to only 47% of the Viggen's.

A joint British-French project, the Concorde was the world's first supersonic airliner, making its maiden flight in 1977. Carrying 128 passengers, the aircraft flies at a height of 16,000 m (52,500 ft), crossing the Atlantic in about 3 hours at a speed of 2,330 km/h (1,450 mph).

Saab 105

Ragnar Härdmark was first involved in the design of the 21R and 32 Lansen aircraft. During the 1960s, he became Project Leader for the Saab 105, before transferring to Car Division to undertake development work.

According to the designer, the 105 was to have "no curves whatever, except where absolutely necessary" to facilitate its production. The A60 version pictured below provides the proof!

When Saab commenced design work on Aircraft 105 in April 1960, the Company's marketing specialists were confident that they could also sell a civilian version of the plane. Given the prevailing climate of optimism and the cheapness of aviation fuel, there appeared to be no reason why harassed European businessmen should not soon be flying the Continent in corporate aircraft, as their American counterparts had been doing for years.

However, the picture changed completely when the Swedish Air Force got wind of the Company's plans; the flying school at Ljungbyhed needed a new trainer and the 105 was the perfect answer. (The fact that the plane could also be adapted for strike missions was a further advantage.) In the event, the Air Force decided to order a total of 150 aircraft.

The initial test flight took place on 29 June 1963. In the Sk60 — the 2-seater version bought by the Air Force — the instructor and pupil were seated side by side. However, the two ejection seats could easily be replaced by four conventional seats to convert the plane into a fast liaison aircraft.

Another version, the Sk60C, was equipped with a panoramic camera mounted in the nose, with a built-in flash unit for night photography.

The high-wing configuration made the 105 ideal as a weapons carrier. The speed and climbing performance of the armed version (the 105XT) — which was equipped with a much more powerful engine, together with an advanced navigation and sighting system — was superior even to that of the 'Flying Barrel'.

No 105s were, in fact, ever built for civilian use, probably due to the fact that being a twin-engined plane, a two-man crew was required by safety regulations. This was obviously an unreasonably expensive means of flying only two passengers.

Although the Swedish Air Force purchased most of the 105s built by Saab, forty of the later 105XTs were sold to the Austrian Air Force under the designation 105ÖE.

Despite strenuous efforts on the part of the Sales Department to sell the plane in other countries, these were effectively blocked by Government regulations restricting exports of war matériel.

The Sk60 is an easy-to-manage aircraft in most respects. Refuelling and rearming between missions can be accomplished in 12 minutes by two conscripts with limited training.

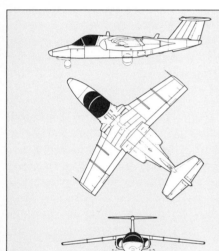

Saab 105 Sk60

Training, light strike, reconnaissance and staff liaison aircraft

Versions	Sk60A, A60B, Sk60C, Sk60D, Sk60E, 105G/OE		
Engine type/thrust	Sk60	RM9 Turbomeca Aubisque/2×743 kgf (2×1638 lbf)	
	105	General Electric J85−17B/2×1293 kgf (2×2851 lbf)	

	Sk60A/D/E	B/C	105G/OE
Span, m (ft)	9.5 (31'2¼")	9.5 (31'2¼")	9.5 (31'2¼")
Length, m (ft)	10.5 (34'5½")	B=10.5 (34'5½")	10.5 (34'5½")
		C=11.0 (36'1")	
Take-off weight, kg (lb)	4050 (8929)	4500 (9921)	6500 (14330)
Maximum/cruising speed, km/h	770/640	765/640	970/800
(mph)	(478/398)	(475/398)	(603/497)
Landing speed, km/h (mph)	165 (103)	165 (103)	165 (103)
Range, km (miles)	1940 (1210)	1780 (1110)	2750 (1710)
Max. altitude, m (ft)	13500 (44290)	12000 (39370)	13700 (44950)

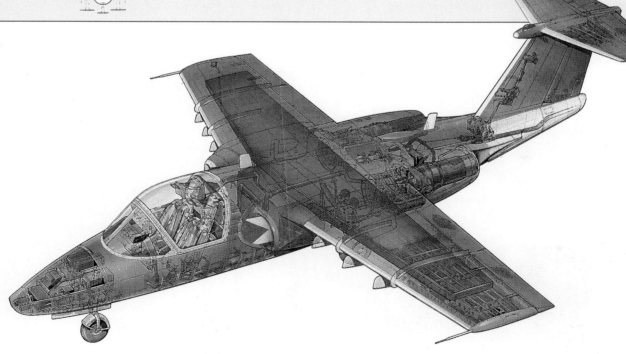

Saab Sonett

Produced exclusively for rallying, only six specimens of the attractive 1956 Saab Sonett (I) were built.

The Saab Sonett III (the lines successfully refined) was produced up to 1974. The grille-mounted spotlamps were optional extras. When not in use, the headlamps were retracted into the body.

Although Saab's standard production models had acquitted themselves well in Swedish rallies, they were not quite up to international standards, especially since the competition rules of the early 50s did not permit special modification.

Saab created a sensation at the important Stockholm Motor Show in 1956 with the introduction of a sports roadster named the Sonett. However, far from being an ordinary road model, the new car was designed exclusively for the major rally circuits.

Built on an advanced aluminum box-section frame, the car was powered by the 3-cylinder engine from the 93, modified to deliver 57.5 hp compared with the 33 hp developed by the standard unit. The result was a successful combination of low weight and high strength. The engine was mounted behind the transmission, the direction of rota-

tion being reversed to give three forward speeds.

The body was made of fiberglass-reinforced plastic (a completely new material at the time) – and the complete car weighed a mere 500 kg (1,100 lb).

With a top speed of 160 km/h (just 100 mph) and capable of covering a kilometer in 36 seconds from a standing start, the new model was more than a match for its competitors. Fitted with a hard top and a 4-speed transmission, it was capable of 180 km/h (112 mph). The initial series consisted of 6 cars and the model was also entered in a number of track events. In time, however, the rules of rallying were altered to permit the entry of modified production models – and, overnight, the old 93 once more became competitive. The Sonett had had its day! Two of the original 6 models are now on display in the Saab Museum. Three more are owned by collectors, while the sixth was written off following a crash.

Although Saab had never really abandoned the idea of producing a sports car, it had its doubts when Malmö Flygindustri (MFI) announced its intention of building one, the MFI 13, using standard Saab components, in the early. However, circumstances persuaded the Company to change its mind and an initial series of 25 cars was built (almost entirely by hand) while proper manufacturing facilities were being established. Although intended for showing at an exhibition in New York, the first Sonett II was completed ahead of schedule, and the model was unveiled in Stockholm in 1966.

The original shape of the MFI 13 survived, a longer front end being the only major modification. Since the entire front could be opened, the car was exceptionally easy to service. Equipped with triple carburetors, the engine (from the Saab 96 Monte Carlo) developed 60 hp. The first series was fitted with a 2-cycle engine which was later superseded by the new 4-cycle, V4 unit introduced in the 96. However, this modification caused an unsightly bulge in the hood which spoiled the lines of the car.

Since this was only one of several features which detracted from its appearance, the model was restyled by two designers (Swedish and Italian) after it had been in production for a couple of years, resulting in radical alteration of the lines. The new version (known

as the Sonett III) was completed in Spring 1970, and 740 cars were produced in the first year. Although the opening front section had, unfortunately, been eliminated (making service more difficult), compensation was provided in the form of a larger trunk. The car was later fitted with a self-repairing bumper which, however, did not make it more attractive. The next innovation was the equipment of the 1974 model (the last of the series) with headlamp wipers. Throughout the V4 period, the car was fitted with a standard engine. Apart from the inherent qualities of the design, its sporty characteristics were attributable to the enhanced performance permitted by the low weight of 770 kg (1,700 lb). In total, 10,219 Saab Sonett IIs and IIIs were built.

The complete Sonett family. From left: the Sonett I, the Catherina and MFI 13 prototypes, the Sonett II and the Sonett III.

The entire front of the Sonett I and II could be opened, making the cars exceptionally easy to service.

Saab Sonett, 1966–1974

1966 model (I)
Length/width/height: 377/144/111 cm (148/57/44 in)
Three-cylinder, 2-cycle, 841-cm³, 60-hp, longitudinally mounted engine
Four-speed transmission with freewheel and column-mounted gearshift
Independent suspension, coil springs front and rear
Disc brakes at front, drum brakes at rear, parking brake acting on rear wheels
Top speed: approx. 150 km/h (93 mph)

1967 model (II)
V4, 4-cycle, 1,498-cm³, 65-hp, longitudinally mounted engine
Top speed: approx. 160 km/h (99 mph)

1970 model (III)
Length/width/height: 390/150/119 cm (154/59/47 in)
Four-cylinder, 4-cycle, 1498-cm³, 65-hp, longitudinally mounted engine
Four-speed transmission with freewheel and floor-mounted gearshift
Independent suspension, coil springs front and rear
Disc brakes at front, drum brakes at rear, parking brake acting on rear wheels
Top speed: approx. 165 km/h (103 mph)

1971 model
1,698-cm³ engine

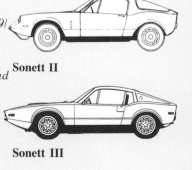

Sonett II

Sonett III

1964 — SAAB JOINS THE 'BILLION CLUB'

For the first time, the Group's combined sales passed the billion-kronor mark, totaling SKr 1,106 million ($220 million).

Unease was abroad in the aircraft sector. Despite pressure from Saab, the Government had not made a decision on the Viggen project — which was worth about SKr 9 billion ($1.8 billion) at that time. In response to the Company's reminder that approximately 1,000 employees would become redundant if the project did not materialize, the Ministry of Defense wrote: "The eventual necessity of laying off employees is entirely a matter for Saab management. In procuring matériel for defense purposes, it is not the function of the Ministry to provide employment".

Despite this harsh tone, the Matériel Administration placed a series of orders worth over SKr 360 million ($72 million) for the 35 Draken, the RB08 missile and further development work on the 37 Viggen.

However, Saab was also reaching for the stars. Working in collaboration with Asea and LM Ericsson, Saab engineers (under the direction of Ove Hammarström) started work on the design of a satellite for scientific studies. The project was carried out under the auspices of the European Space Research Organization (ESRO). Launching was scheduled for 1967.

Shortage of labor was a further problem and, in an attempt to remedy the situation, personnel officers were dispatched on recruiting trips to northern Sweden. (The Company required 500 skilled workers every year.)

Despite its exotic connotations, Uruguay was an interesting market for Saab cars. An assembly plant was established in Montevideo, both as a means of supplying the local demand and gaining a foothold in the Latin American free trade area (whose General Secretariat was located in the city).

The demand was so great that Brynolf Holmqvist, the Swedish engineering manager, was often obliged to intervene when buyers attempted to persuade sales personnel to deliver cars before they had been completely finished or inspected. Operations continued for several years until the Uruguayan market collapsed for political and economic reasons.

1965 — Saab BECOMES SAAB

Although Svenska Aeroplan Aktiebolaget had long been known as Saab, it was impractical to use one name while being known by another. Furthermore, the original name no longer described all of the Company's activities. The National Patent and Registration Office was, therefore, advised of the Company's intention of changing its name to SAAB Aktiebolag.

Following some controversy regarding the project, Parliament resolved that "development work on the 37 Viggen aircraft, including the manufacture of a certain number of prototypes, is to be completed". However, the Government not only postponed production for 18 months, but reduced the number of aircraft. Nevertheless, Tryggve Holm commented in a press interview: "I am still glad that we have come so far — you might say that we have won the first round. We at Saab appreciate the acclaim which the Viggen has received."

On the other hand, deliveries of the Saab 105 commenced according to plan.

A supplementary agreement, detailing a number of more explicit definitions and changes concerning the status of sub-contractors in relation to Saab as main

The severe winter of 1965—66 provided an additional cold-starting test for the cars which awaited delivery. All passed with flying colors!

contractor, was concluded with the Matériel Administration. In conjunction with this, the main agreement was extended until the end of 1975.

A workshop for the repair and reconditioning of bodies, engines and gearboxes was established in Kristinehamn.

Work on a sports car with a reinforced-plastic body was commenced in association with AB Malmö Flygindustri (MFI) and AB Svenska Järnvägsverkstäderna (ASJ) — a response to pressure from the USA, where the potential publicity value of an elegant sports model was considered sufficient to justify its production "even if it did not make a profit". Sales of 3,600 cars were expected to cover the development costs. The model was christened the Sonett II.

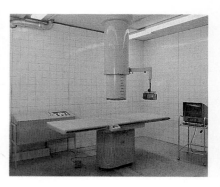

Saab's new company logo.

1966 — TOWARDS THE STARS

Times were tough for automakers. At Saab, production was cut by 20%. The 2-cycle engine had had its day and a successor was needed — a problem which remained to be solved. After testing a wide variety of alternatives, the Saab engineers eventually opted for a German-built Ford V4 unit. Although Ford had not achieved particular success with the engine, Saab realized that it possessed excellent potential for further development.

The 100,000th export model — a Saab 95 station wagon — was delivered to the Middle East.

The first prototype of the Sonett II was unveiled to the press in February. Although a pre-production series of 25 cars was under manufacture, no decision had been taken to commence production proper.

The Company's computers were obviously producing the correct results, to judge by a memorandum from the Board stating that "computer production may offset the expected fall-off in military orders".

The major event of the year was the launch of the Viggen, although it was to be some time before the plane took to the air. According to the comprehensive test schedule, flight testing was not due to commence until 1967.

In partnership with British, French and German companies, Saab formed a space technology group known as MESH, within which the member companies operated as independent entities and assignments were to be allocated according to resources in terms of knowhow and available capacity. The structure was not unlike that of AB Förenade Flygverkstäder which Saab had formed with ASJA in the early days.

The development of medical X-ray equipment was commenced in 1966. The equipment was manufactured alternately at Jönköping and in the robot department at Linköping until the operation was sold off in 1984.

Assembly of a Saab RB05 guided missile designed for use against marine and ground targets.

Saab 99

The Saab 99 was unveiled in November 1967, the first owners taking delivery of their cars (the 1969 model) a year later. The 99 signified the start of the move towards bigger cars.

From 1970 on, the Saab 99 was also available in a 4-door version. The 1970 model also featured an 87-hp fuel-injected engine and an automatic transmission.

In an earlier history of Saab cars, the author observed: "Now firmly established in a number of markets, the marque is here to stay". However, competition was becoming tougher — and the Company realized that it was time to start developing a completely new model designed to attract a wide circle of potential buyers while retaining its market appeal for a considerable period ahead. The result was the launching of Project Gudmund on 2 April 1965 (the codename being taken from the Swedish name-day calendar). It was exactly 20 years since the preliminary sketches of the very first Saab had been produced.

Nicknamed the 'Toad', the first 'Gudmund prototype' took to the Swedish roads in 1966.

The car consisted of a 96 body, widened by 20 cm (8 in) and mounted on a 99 floor-pan. The body of the 96 was ideal for hiding the transition from the 3-cylinder, 2-cycle engine to the new 4-cylinder, 4-cycle unit; plenty of space was available under the hood. However, it was impossible to test individual components and systems for the new model in ordinary 96s. Since new designs had to be road-tested — a function requiring a complete chassis, including engine and other auxiliaries — the 'Toad' was built to deceive a curious press. Despite this, it was not long before the deception was exposed.

The codename Gudmund became redundant on 22 November 1967 when the new

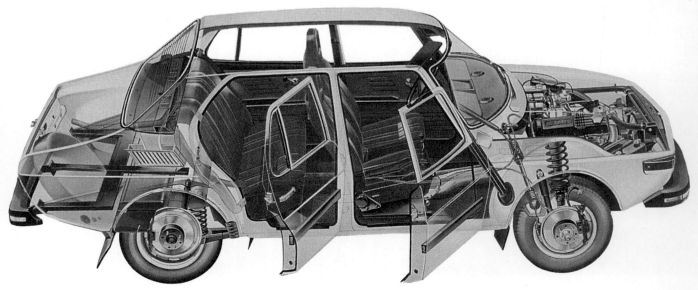

model – the Saab 99 – was introduced to the press in Stockholm. The design was the product of 400,000 'engineer-hours' and a test program of vastly greater scope than that undergone by any previous Saab.

However, the car did not become available to ordinary buyers until Fall 1968, as the 1969 model. In the interim, it was driven (under strictly controlled conditions) only by Saab personnel and by certain selected customers, all of whom were obliged to file regular reports on its performance. Broadly-based testing of this nature is frequently used by small, specialized automakers in preparation for full-scale production of a new model.

The first version of the 99 (a 2-door model)

Maximum safety under winter conditions is ensured by Saab's front-wheel drive and 15" wheels.

The 1971 model was equipped with headlamp wipers and washers – a safety feature which later became a legal requirement.

Saab 99, 1967–1984/Saab 90, 1985–

Length/width/height: 435/167/144 cm (171/66/57 in)
Four-cylinder, 4-cycle, 1,709-cm³, 80-hp, longitudinally mounted engine
Four-speed transmission (freewheel until 1970) with floor-mounted gearshift
Independent suspension, coil springs front and rear
Disc brakes all round with parking brake acting on front wheels
Top speed: approx. 145 km/h (90 mph)

1970 model
Automatic transmission as option

1971 model
1,854-cm³, 86 or 95-hp engines as options

1972 model
Length: 445 cm (175 in)
1,985-cm³, 110-hp engine as option (EMS model)
Top speed: 155 km/h (96 mph)

1975 model
1,985-cm³, 100, 108 or 118-hp engine

1978 model
145-hp engine (Turbo)
Top speed: 195 km/h (121 mph)

1982 model
Five-speed transmission

1985 model
Saab 99 becomes Saab 90

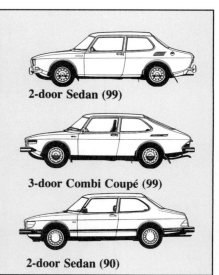

2-door Sedan (99)

3-door Combi Coupé (99)

2-door Sedan (90)

Buyers of the 1970 model had the option of an automatic transmission. The Saab 99 was of more or less the same generation as another advanced Saab product — the Viggen fighter plane.

was available only with a 1,709-cm³ engine rated at 80 hp. The car was also equipped with disc brakes all round.

Sales in Sweden totaled 19,411 in the very first year of production, placing the 99 fifth in terms of new registrations.

The customary program of development and improvement undergone by the model during the succeeding years culminated in a major advance with the 1977 launch of the Saab 99 Turbo — a project which had naturally been surrounded by a formidable veil of secrecy. Although Saab had already experi-

mented with turbochargers in its rally cars, these activities had been discontinued to avoid the disclosure of future developments in production models. The new rally version, known as the Saab 99 Turbo Rally, was introduced officially on 16 January 1978. In this case, although the original engine rating was raised from 145 to 240 hp, the increase in engine torque to 369 Nm (273 lb ft) at 3,500 r/min was the most dramatic innovation.

Shortly after, however, the competition rules were modified to allow the entry of specials (only 200 of which had to be built to

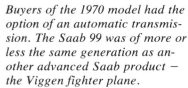

The Swedish-built 2-liter engine was used in the 99 from 1971 on. This model was also fitted with a unique self-repairing bumper.

The Saab 99 finally provided the key to the American market, although the square headlamps were not approved. Despite the Trollhättan registration, the model in the picture is fitted with US headlamps.

obtain approval) and Saab — regarding the trend in developments as undesirable — withdrew from competition in 1980.

The 1985 model underwent such comprehensive modification that the car was renamed the Saab 90. Among other changes, the rear end of the model was now of the same design as the 900 Sedan, while the engine was designed to use unleaded gasoline. The car was earmarked mainly for the Scandinavian and western European markets.

At this juncture, total production of the 99 had reached 590,000.

Although the Saab 99 retained its basic lines for many years after 1969, the Combi Coupé body introduced in 1974 afforded buyers a wide choice of variants. The new body combined the elegance of a sedan with the spaciousness of a station wagon.

The rear of the 1985 99 was so drastically restyled that the model was renamed the Saab 90.

1967 — A CHANGE OF PACE

Curt Mileikowsky
President of Saab, 1967—1970
President of Scania-Vabis, 1969—
1970
President of Saab-Scania, 1970—
1978

Although many observers believed it would never happen, Saab finally forsook the 2-cycle engine. The Ford V4 engine which Saab had modified for use in the 95 and 96 became an instant success. After testing the engine just before he retired from the rally scene, Erik Carlsson reported: "All of a sudden, we had 30 more horsepower under the bonnet — not to mention thousands of revs with real pulling power. With the V4, I was able, for the first time, to take my foot off the throttle driving downhill — the car seemed incredibly fast". The success of the engine was such that Ford advertised its Taunus 12M as a "Ford with a Saab engine".

Henrik Gustavsson, Saab's Technical Director at the time, once said: "As an extremely small automaker in international terms, Saab cannot afford to make mistakes. Therefore, it is vital that our product development work be properly directed and that every modification, every improvement, should be fully justified — and preferably of an innovative nature". The innovative spirit was apparent when the Saab 99 was introduced in November. In an article on the model, the American magazine 'Car and Driver' reported: "Saab does not make cars — it makes Saabs — models offering a highly distinctive and particularly logical solution to at least one of man's transport problems".

As the first stage in the biggest program ever undertaken by the Swedish Defense Forces, the Viggen made its maiden flight on 8 February, one week ahead of schedule.

The newly formed MESH Group received its first order for two research satellites from the European Space Research Organization (ESRO), a contract worth a total of SKr 115 million ($23 million). The satellites were intended for the study of stellar astronomy, cosmic radiation and the effects of high sunspot activity.

It had been an eventful year for Tryggve Holm as he stepped down from the job of President in favor of Dr. Curt Mileikowsky. By this time, the Trollhättan plant had become so large that the messenger girls had been given scooters!

The Saab 99 was unveiled at a ceremony in Stockholm on Wednesday, 22 November 1967. However, series production did not commence until nearly a year later, the intervening period being used for public test driving.

1968 − MERGER

On 5 April, the Ministry of Defense issued a communiqué commencing with the statement: "At today's meeting, the Cabinet approved the order of 175 Viggen aircraft (interceptor and training version), delivery of the last 75 to be conditional on the decision of Parliament. Based on a total of 175 aircraft, the value of the contract with Saab will be of the order of SKr 1,690 million ($338 million)".

Another, much smaller, yet significant deal merited a brief mention in the minutes of a Board meeting. It read: "Saab has acquired the total shareholding in Malmö Flygindustri (MFI) for SKr 800,000 ($160,000)". MFI was one of the first companies in Europe to manufacture reinforced plastic products, including gliders, canoes and boats. In the 50s, the company had also begun to design and develop small powered aircraft.

On Friday 20 December, the dailies announced with banner headlines: "Huge Wallenberg merger − Saab buys Scania-Vabis. Bombshell for 23,000 employees − We knew nothing −".

The Annual Report for the year was a little more restrained: "A significant volume of exports, over and above sales to the obviously highly important domestic market, is a prerequisite to the future development of the Swedish automotive industry. Success will demand intensive market and product development, a context in which the Scandinavian market, in particular, will play a crucial role.

On this basis, the Boards of Saab Aktiebolag and AB Scania-Vabis decided, at year's end, to propose a merger between the companies, to create the conditions which will enable the resources of both to be utilized more effectively, particularly in the areas of research, product development, production and export sales".

In some circles, however, the news of Sweden's largest-ever takeover (the total value of which was about SKr 800 million or $160 million) failed even to raise eyebrows. Industry Minister Krister Wickman commented merely: "I know nothing about the deal. In any case, it is mainly the concern of the Wallenberg family".

Valmet, the state-owned Finnish company, had long been examining the viability of producing cars locally. In the face of the stiffest possible competition, Saab was chosen as a partner in the venture. A new plant was built at Uusikaupunki and production (initially 15,000 cars per year) was scheduled to commence by the end of 1969.

Major progress was also made in the computer sector with the sale of thirty D21 installations and the receipt of orders for seven of the new D22 version. Divisional management maintained that "the Swedish-built computers supplied to the county councils have proved themselves superior to the IBM machines".

Comprehensive reorganization of Saab's operations was undertaken to rationalize the use of all available human and technical resources, the Company being divided into autonomous, product-oriented divisions, each responsible for its own profitability and provided with its own organizational structure.

The activities of the new divisions were aircraft; missiles, space and avionics; medical technology; industrial control systems and equipment; computers; electronics and cars.

Marcus Wallenberg was elected Chairman of the Board of the new Company.

The operator's panel for the Saab D21 with the tape station in the background. As one of the fastest and most compact machines on the market, the machine could add 100,000 six-digit numbers per second.

Oy Saab-Valmet AB
Valmet spent a number of years seeking a partner to establish a car-production plant in Finland as a joint venture. Saab-Scania was chosen in competition with several other European automakers and the two parties signed an agreement in 1968. Equally owned by Saab-Scania and Oy Valmet AB, the new company (known as Saab-Valmet) became the largest industrial project ever undertaken between Sweden and Finland. Expanded in several stages, the plant employed 2,300 people in 1986, in which year it produced 44,000 cars.

Scania-Vabis

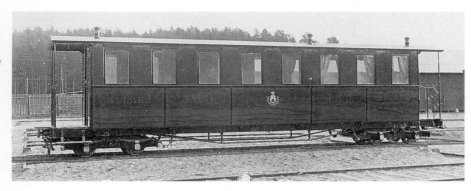

A VABIS railway car ready for delivery from the Södertälje works.

Journeyman coachbuilder David Ekenberg was a little more far-sighted than most of his contemporaries. Having established a successful coachbuilding business in Södertälje in 1823, he was in an ideal position to make a rapid transition from making horse-drawn coaches to building rail carriages when the Government of the day decided to construct a national railroad system in the mid-1850s. (Truth to tell, the transition was not a major one.)

Ekenberg was not allowed to monopolize this lucrative trade; in Stockholm, AB Atlas had also embarked on the manufacture of rail carriages. However, Atlas made slow progress, and becoming aware of Ekenberg's successful operation, made an offer for the complete concern. This was accepted and production was transferred to Stockholm, the

staff who made the move including Philip Wersén, an engineer and a relation of Ekenberg. Eventually becoming homesick for Södertälje, Wersén succeeded in persuading Surahammars Bruk (another company which had begun to manufacture rolling stock) to open a factory in the town. Founded in 1891, the new company rejoiced in the name of Vagnfabriksaktiebolaget i Södertelge, or VABIS. However, relations between Wersén and the Board soured after a year, and the former left to establish his own company (in the same trade).

Realizing that the market for rolling stock would soon be over-supplied, the management of Vabis began to seek an alternative product. Deciding on the automobile – the symbol of the new age – the company dispatched one of its engineers, Gustaf Erikson, to England and France to study the new technological marvel.

Erikson was obviously convinced that the car would make an ideal complement to the railroad, and the first VABIS car (designed by himself) appeared in 1897. Burning kerosene (since Erikson considered gasoline too dangerous), the model was powered by two horizontal cylinders.

The company's judgment was correct and the first VABIS truck – a 1.5-tonne model powered by a 9-hp V2 engine – appeared in

The first VABIS motor vehicle. In Fall 1903, the truck was to be seen on the streets of Stockholm.

1902. (By now, the designers had overcome their fear of gasoline and had abandoned kerosene.)

The truck attracted major attention at the first Swedish International Motor Exhibition in 1903. It was not, however, the only truck on view, the other being a competitor from Skåne (or Scania) in the south of Sweden.

In the early 1890s, a British company had used its Swedish agent to establish a bicycle factory in Malmö, and Maskinfabriksaktiebolaget Scania was formed in 1900 to continue the production of these velocipedes. The management of this concern was also quick to realize that the future lay in automobiles, producing its first model as early as in 1901. Although the first engines were purchased abroad, those fitted in models from 1903 on were of Scania's own design.

Competition between Scania and Vabis might have been described as 'cordial', the threat from across the Atlantic being much more serious. And although the truck sector had been relatively 'peaceful' for several years, neither of the companies possessed the resources to meet the challenge which was certain to develop in that area also. The logical step was taken in Spring 1911 with the merger of the two under the title of Scania-Vabis — a name which the group retained until 1969.

The manufacture of engines, cars and light trucks was concentrated in Södertälje, with the production of heavy trucks and fire engines in Malmö.

Success appears to have followed quickly, particularly in the export market, and agents were soon appointed not only in Norway, Finland, Denmark and Holland, but in far-flung parts of the globe such as Russia and Australia.

Trucks were the main export. As expected,

The 'Erikson automobile' on a trial run at Surahammar in 1897.

The new Scania bicycles appeared in 1900.

The first Scania truck was equipped with a 2-cylinder, 4-cycle engine rated at 10—12 hp.

The first 'genuine' Scania-Vabis bus (built on a purpose-designed bus chassis) was introduced in 1911.

the market for cars had become considerably tougher and Scania-Vabis was forced to abandon their production in 1924, the Malmö factory being closed down a couple of years later.

All production activities, including engine manufacture, were transferred to the Södertälje plant, the resultant concentration of available resources laying the foundation for the company's development over the coming decades.

Scania-Vabis also had a long tradition in building buses, the first of which was delivered to Nordmarkens Automobil Trafik AB in 1911.

Although demand naturally fell during the First World War, a development which occurred between the wars had the effect of making Scania-Vabis the leader in this area also. The event was the delivery, in 1922, of the first mail bus which not only carried mail, goods and passengers, but also operated as a snowplow along its route. Another major advance was the appearance, in 1932, of the 'bulldog' bus in which the engine was mounted above the front axle and the full width of the body extended right to the front, with the driver seated to one side. The demand for this type was so huge that more buses than trucks were built during most of the 30s.

The Company pursued development work on its own engines in parallel with its vehicle-building activities. Work on a 110-hp aircraft engine for the Royal Swedish Air Force was commenced in 1916, while the first attempts to adapt a Scania-Vabis engine to burn diesel fuel took place between 1925 and 1927. The first series of Hesselman diesel units, developing about 80 hp, was produced in 1931, and the first diesel engine of the Company's own design (featuring a pre-combustion chamber) appeared in 1936. This was superseded, in 1948, by the direct-injection engine, which was destined to achieve a worldwide reputation for unsurpassed fuel economy, reliability and life.

Although mass-produced trucks accounted for most of the company's turnover, facilities for retooling in order to produce special vehicles of various types (such as fire engines, military vehicles and all-wheel drive vehicles) were introduced at an early stage. Large

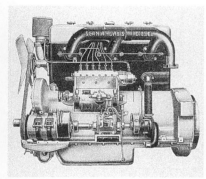

The first diesel engine of the Company's own design was built in 1936.

The 'bulldog' bus – a completely new design. The year was 1932.

numbers of terrain vehicles and tanks were produced during the Second World War.

By the end of the Second World War in 1945, annual production was running at over 1,500 chassis – a fivefold increase over 1939. Transportation systems throughout Europe were more or less in ruins and the demand for both trucks and buses was enormous. Orders streamed in and the Södertälje plant was expanded in several stages. Production was trebled within ten years, over half the output being exported.

In 1948, Scania-Vabis became general agent for Volkswagen in Sweden, an event which was to be of crucial importance in establishing a national dealer network and in obtaining capital for investment in plant, research and export marketing.

Major penetration of the international market was achieved during the 50s and 60s, exports of trucks and buses increasing from 17% to 70%.

This period also witnessed intensive product development work. Mass production of a completely new range of trucks based on a 165-hp, 6-cylinder diesel engine commenced in 1958, followed by the next generation in 1968 and the introduction of a 350-hp, V8 engine in 1969.

Notable among the company's buses were the 1953 Metropol, 1955 Capitol and 1966 CR 76 (all rear-engined), and the 1959 CF 75 front-engined model.

Major capital investment projects included a central laboratory and test track (built in

1964), a press shop at Luleå and a chassis-assembly shop at Södertälje, both built in 1967.

Production plants were also built in the Netherlands and Brazil.

In 1968, the Boards of Scania-Vabis and Saab proposed a merger "to create the conditions which will enable the resources of both companies to be utilized more effectively, particularly in the areas of research, product development, production and export sales" (the quotation being taken from Saab's Annual Report for that year). The step was finally approved by the annual general meetings of Scania-Vabis, Nordarmatur and Saab in 1969.

During the Second World War, Scania-Vabis produced light tanks and artillery carriers at Södertälje.

An L71 on the Argentinian pampas. The truck was used in making a film about Scania-Vabis in 1956.

Saab 37 Viggen

The unconventional twin-delta configuration, featuring a canard wing above and ahead of the main wing, affords maximum top speed, minimum vulnerability to turbulence and low landing speed. The JA37 is armed with a built-in 30-mm cannon, as well as Sidewinder and Sky Flash missiles.

"In planning its air defenses, every nation must define the most likely threat to its security in the 15, or even 20 years immediately ahead". The quotation − from a brochure published by Saab to introduce the Viggen − illustrates the nature of the long-term planning framework within which modern aircraft designers must work.

Studies aimed at developing a successor to the Draken were carried out between 1952 and 1957. The aircraft configuration and engine were specified in 1960, and the navigation system was selected the next year. Construction commenced in 1964, the first prototype making its maiden flight in 1967. Saab received the initial order for production aircraft a year later and in 1972 − 20 years after the start of the project − the first operational squadron was established at F7 Wing in Såtenäs. Given the course of events, it might be surmised that the Saab engineers of the 50s were equipped with crystal balls!

The brochure stressed that "long-term strategic planning is imperative, given the service life expected of equipment requiring such an enormous capital investment". In an attempt to minimize the development costs, the Saab designers first proposed to modernize the still relatively serviceable Draken by installing a new engine, new electronics and new armament. However, the plane being a generation too old, it was considered too difficult to adapt it to the new requirements.

For economic reasons, emphasis was placed on the design of a multi-role aircraft

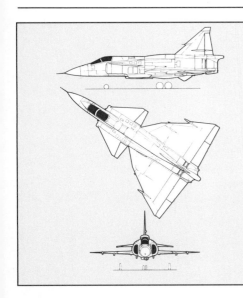

Saab 37 Viggen

Strike, training, reconnaissance and interceptor aircraft

Versions	AJ37, Sk37, SF37, SH37, JA37
Engine type/thrust	AJ37-SH37 RM8A Svenska Flygmotor/Pratt & Whitney JT8D-22/ 6700−11800 kgf (14771−26014 lbf)
	JA37 RM8B Svenska Flygmotor/Pratt & Whitney JT8D-22/7300− 12750 kgf (16093−28108 lbf)

	AJ, Sk, SF, SH	JA
Span, m (ft)	10.6 (34'9¼")	10.6 (34'9¼")
Length, m (ft)	16.3 (53'5¾")	16.4 (53'9¾")
Take-off weight, kg (lb)	16000 (35273)	17000−23000 (37478−50705)
Maximum/cruising speed, Mach	2+/0.9	2+/0.9
Landing speed, km/h (mph)	220 (137)	220 (137)
Range, km (miles)	2000 (1240) plus	2000 (1240) plus
Max. altitude, m (ft)	18000 (59060)	18000 (59060)

for interceptor, strike and reconnaissance missions. With supersonic performance as an obvious prerequisite, the plane was also to be capable of operating from highway bases.

These apparently contradictory specifications were finally reconciled by adopting a twin-delta, canard wing configuration.

In the mid-60s, strategists − and especially economists − in many parts of the world were examining the feasibility of replacing manned aircraft by missiles. However, Sweden's defense experts decided (partly on the basis of military econonomic analyses) that

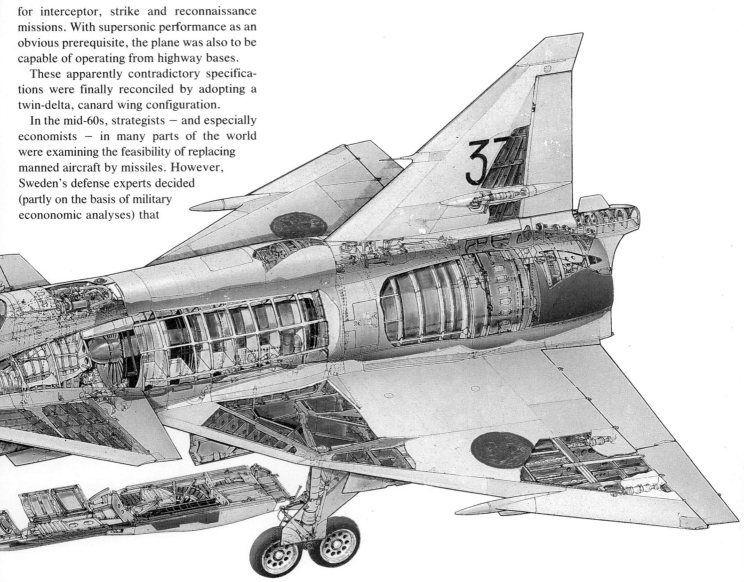

The picture is proof of the Viggen's superb flying qualities. The pilot has virtually parked the nose of the aircraft on the ramp of the Hercules transport on which the photographer is standing.

the nation's air power would be based largely on manned aircraft in the foreseeable future.

Nevertheless, the Viggen was regarded not merely as an individual aircraft but – in combination with STRIL 60 (the Swedish Air Defense Control System) – as an integral part of a coordinated weapons system. Within the system, the aircraft was to be a 'platform' capable of being transformed into any one of five different versions, each assigned a specific role.

The first of these was the AJ 37. Designed

as a strike aircraft with a secondary role as an interceptor, this version made its first flight in 1967.

Deliveries of the Sk37 2-seater trainer commenced in 1972. This aircraft was also designed for a limited strike role.

Development work on two reconnaissance versions commenced in 1968. The first of these, designated the SH37, left the production line in 1974, replacing the S32C Lansen. The SH37 was fitted with photographic equipment and jamming-resistant radar for

Readying the plane for a new mission can be accomplished by conscript personnel. Led by a chief technician, five men can prepare the Viggen for its next take-off in ten minutes.

reconnaissance at sea. (The letters SH are an acronym for the term 'naval reconnaissance' in Swedish.) Delivered a year later, the second version (which replaced the S35 Draken) was known as the SF37, and carried camera equipment instead of radar in the nose. (The letters SF used in this case stood for 'photographic reconnaissance'.)

The JA37 interceptor version – an all-weather defense aircraft designed especially for low-altitude operations – appeared in 1975. The engine featured an additional fan

stage, while the on-board equipment was supplemented by pulse-Doppler radar, a 30-mm cannon and advanced avionics. The JA37 also possesses strike capability.

The Viggen was the largest single project yet undertaken for the Swedish defense forces. All of the major sub-systems used in the aircraft were developed and/or produced by Swedish companies. Saab-Scania was appointed main contractor, assisted by a joint coordinating body representative of all the industries involved.

The JA37 is one of the most versatile and advanced interceptors in the world. The on-board computer is programmed with imaginary weapons for carrying out tactical exercises. The 'missiles' behave as though primed and the 'cannon' as though loaded, enabling the pilot to select the appropriate weapon and to simulate various types of attack.

The Viggen can land on a straight 500-meter stretch of road and can take off using an even shorter run.

1969–1971

In 1969, Saab-Scania started to install electronic control systems in 'Permobil' invalid cars in newly-fitted premises at Stensholm.

1969 – CAUSE AND EFFECT

As expected, the merger between Saab and Scania-Vabis was approved by the AGMs of the two companies. Nordarmatur — a company which produced process control equipment and operated a large-scale foundry (a facility for which Saab-Scania had excellent use) — was also incorporated in the Group.

In April, Gösta Nilsson resigned as President of Scania-Vabis. He was succeeded by Curt Mileikowsky, already President of Saab.

The first aircraft built by newly acquired MFI (the MFI-15) completed its flight tests successfully, while another newcomer to the Saab family also gave birth to its first-born, in the shape of a Saab 96 which rolled off the assembly line at the Saab-Valmet plant at Uusikaupunki, Finland. Scania was no less active in launching new products, introducing three forward-control trucks (the LB80, 85 and 140), as well as the Metro-Scania bus. The 140 was equipped with the new Scania DS 114 350-hp diesel engine, making it the most powerful road vehicle in Europe. At this time, the last bus chassis left the assembly line at Södertälje and production was transferred, in its entirety, to the Katrineholm plant.

Unveiled at the International Air Show in Paris, the Viggen was described in press reports as the major military event of the show.

The 'computer war' finally came to an end when the Government decided that the county councils would install Saab computers only, ordering a further seven installations.

1970 – A NEW NAME

"It was noted that the National Patent and Registration Office sanctioned the registration of SAAB Aktiebolag's new company, known as SAAB-SCANIA Aktiebolag, on 8 June".

The merger also involved major organizational changes. Operations were divided into the following four divisions:

1) Automotive Division — consisting of Scania and Saab cars. Development work was concentrated on environmental aspects such as noise and exhaust emissions, as well as on in-car safety — an area in which rapid adjustment to the imminent introduction of new international and national standards was urgent.

Urho Kekkonen, then President of Finland, officially opened the Saab-Valmet assembly plant at Uusikaupunki in Finland on 13 November 1969.

As on many previous occasions, Saab was the leader in its field. All 1971 models were equipped with the headlamp wipers and washers which it had developed. This feature was later to become legally compulsory in Sweden.

2) Aerospace Division — in which the Viggen was the main project. Plant capacity was stretched to the limit with the production of the Viggen (for Sweden), the Draken (for Denmark and Sweden), the Saab 105 (for Austria) and a number of missiles (also for Sweden), while a serious labor shortage was imposing severe demands on personnel.

3) Computer and Electronics Division — which was completing orders for a number of computer installations, both for stationary applications (such as banks) and mobile applications (such as the Viggen). Other activities of interest included the manufacture of machine tool and industrial process control equipment.

4) Nordarmatur Division — with more than 3,500 products in its range, notably sophisticated instrumentation and fittings for process industry, power stations, liquid pumping installations and ships.

1971 – DIFFICULT TIMES

Sales of Saab-Scania products fell, due to something of a recession in Scandinavia and the rest of Europe.

This created particular difficulties for MFI, which had expected a major order from the Swedish Army for 20 MFI-15 or MFI-17 aircraft for staff operations and liaison duties. The contract was awarded instead to Scottish Aviation, causing the Board of MFI to seriously consider liquidating the company.

In view of the increasing urgency of expanding its activities in the civilian sector, Saab-Scania formed a consortium with the British Aircraft Corporation, Messerschmitt-Bölkow-Blohm and CASA of Spain for the purpose of developing a commercial airliner to be known as the Europlane. Designed to take off and land on short runways, the aircraft was also to have an extremely low noise level. Although the project never came to fruition, the studies yielded valuable experience which was later applied to the design of the SF340.

Having developed considerable expertise in space and satellite technology, Saab-Scania signed an agreement with the Government in December to undertake the joint development of utility satellites for telecommunications and meteorology. Meanwhile, in Australia, the European Space Research Organization launched a space probe carrying equipment designed and manufactured by Saab-Scania.

The headlamp wipers and washers fitted to all 1971 Saabs won the Swedish Automobile Association's annual traffic safety award.

The 1972 Saab 99 was also acclaimed Swedish 'Car of the Year' in recognition of innovations such as its unique self-repairing bumpers.

A workshop was set up in Södertälje to manufacture British engines under license for the 99 and small-scale production was commenced on a trial basis.

All 1971 model Saabs were fitted with headlamp wipers and washers, a traffic safety innovation for which Saab-Scania received a Swedish Automobile Association award.

Safety is the constant watchword of Saab-Scania's designers. A collision test is carried out practically every day in the purpose-built laboratory.

Saab MFI-17 Safari/Supporter

Björn Andreasson, project leader and designer of the MFI-17, was also the inspiration behind a long series of well-known light sports planes and the 'Mule' aircraft. In addition, he was involved in work on the Transporter, which culminated in the design of the SF340.

As the most recent version of the aircraft, the MFI-17TS is powered by a turbocharged engine for improved high-altitude performance.

When Saab acquired Malmö Flygindustri (MFI) in 1968, the Swedish Air Force was beginning to seek a successor to the Sk50 Safir trainer. Furthermore, the Army was planning to replace the Piper L-21Bs which it was using for artillery spotting and liaison operations.

The airplane which MFI had then been developing for some time, and which made its maiden flight on 11 July 1969, promised to be ideal for both of these purposes. The plane could easily be equipped either with a nose wheel (this version being known as the MFI-15A trainer) or with a tail wheel (the artillery spotting version designated MFI-15B). Unfortunately, Saab did not keep themselves fully informed of developments and the Air Force decided to purchase the Beagle Bulldog while the MFI-15 test program was still in progress. Although outstanding test results were achieved, the Army followed suit in the name of standardization.

The capital and operating costs of the aircraft (which was designed specifically for military uses) were so high that only a few civilian customers could possibly have afforded it.

The plane was converted into an efficient weapons carrier by increasing the engine power and making some structural modifications – measures which greatly enhanced its military potential. The new version – the MFI-17 – made its first flight on 6 July 1972. Ironically, the underwing hardpoints on the first aircraft were used by the Swedish aviator, von Rosen, to transport food to the victims of the famine disaster in Ethiopia.

The first purely military version, named the Supporter, was sold to Pakistan (where it is now built under license) in 1974. Further sales to Denmark, Norway and Zambia followed. A civilian version named the Safari was also sold to countries including Norway, Sierra Leone and Ethiopia. Counting both versions, more than 200 of the aircraft were built.

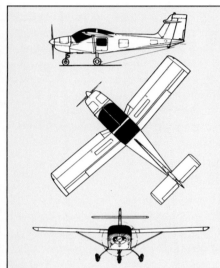

Saab MFI-17 Safari/Supporter

Training, utility and army operations aircraft

Versions	*Safari, Supporter*
Engine type/rating	*Lycoming IO-360/ 200 hp*

	Safari/Supporter
Span, m (ft)	*8.85 (29'0½")*
Length, m (ft)	*7.00 (22'11½")*
Take-off weight, kg (lb)	*1200 (2646)*
Maximum/cruising speed, km/h (mph)	*236/208 (147/129)*
Landing speed, km/h (mph)	*90 (56)*
Range, km (miles)	*1050 (650)*
Max. altitude, m (ft)	*4100 (13540)*

This photograph shows the superb view available to the pilot ahead of the aircraft, as well as above and below the wings.

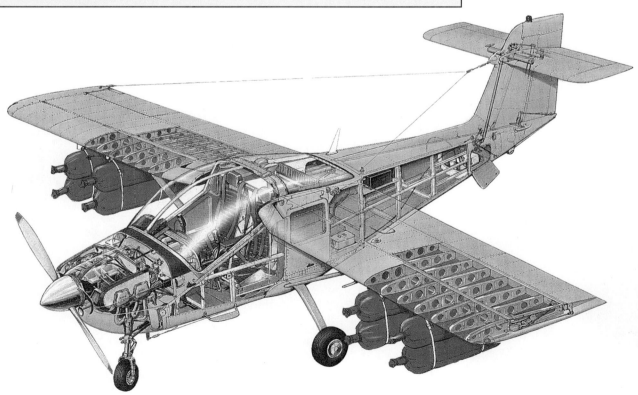

1972-1974

Saab-Scania attaches major importance to sport and recreation, as well as to health and welfare facilities, as part of its personnel programs. The picture shows Sture Malmgren and Gunnar Andersson testing Thore Modigh at the physical training center in Linköping.

1972 — ECHOES FROM THE PAST

The mills of the law ground slowly. Only in September did Södertälje City Court give its assent to the implementation of the merger agreement, adding in its verdict that "Scania-Vabis is hereby deemed to be dissolved and incorporated in Saab-Scania".

The Automotive Division formed as part of the merger was now further divided into the Scania Division and the Saab Car Division.

In Argentina, the domestic truck industry was accorded highly favored treatment. As a protectionist measure, it was decided to exclude foreign producers, although any manufacturer which set up operations before restrictions were imposed would be regarded as 'domestic'. Saab-Scania won the concession in competition with Volvo and Pegaso, the Spanish company, building a new plant at Tucuman to produce buses, trucks and transmissions. The Brazilian plant was also supplied with transmissions from Tucuman.

In February, a research satellite designed to study the Northern Lights was launched from the Esrange base in Kiruna followed, in March, by the launch of a second (TD-1A) from the Vandenberg Air Base outside Los Angeles. Both were built largely from equipment supplied by Saab-Scania.

Another product, which was definitely not intended for space exploration, also made its appearance. This was — of all things — a steam engine. "Saab-Scania is studying the steam engine as an alternative source of motive power for cars; however, no concrete plans to market a steam-driven Saab have yet been made. Even if the findings should prove promising, it would not be feasible to commence production until some time in the 80s".

The steam-driven model is yet to appear.

Experiments were also carried out on anti-lock brakes. At this time, however, the technique was not sufficiently advanced and the costs were excessive. It was to be another 14 years before the feature was finally introduced on production models.

1973 — COMPLETING THE CIRCLE

Ingvar Eriksson
Executive Vice-President, General Manager of Scania Division since 1972

A remarkable circle was completed in October when Saab-Scania acquired a new subsidiary in the form of AB Svenska Järnvägsverkstäderna (ASJ), whose aircraft division had started building airplanes in 1930 and had become part of Saab when the latter was formed later in the decade. At the time, Saab also acquired ASJ's airfield, while ASJ became Saab's largest shareholder. Having wound up many of its activities over the years, ASJ's interests now consisted almost entirely of its foundry operations and industrial estate business (although the Sonett was being manufactured in its plant at Arlöv.) Approximately 90% of the ASJ shareholders accepted Saab-Scania's offer to buy their shares, making the company a wholly-owned subsidiary.

In the spring, Parliament took a far-reaching decision which attracted remarkably little attention, announcing that the Royal Swedish Air Force would henceforth consist of 16 divisions as compared with the 50 or so established in the 1950s — a reduction of about two-thirds. The decision was one which would inevitably have a profound effect on Saab-Scania's future.

Fortunately, however, the Company was now well-established in the civilian market. The first production MFI-15s were delivered in April to Sierra Leone, which also purchased two helicopters. Sales of cars were also excellent, the volume being higher than ever before. With 37,526 registrations, the Company share of the Swedish market was 16.6%, while exports had also risen to a record 52,450 units.

Scania Division reported major progress, as did Datasaab. And, to crown it all, IF Saab's handball team also brought home gold. Although the fortunes of the club have not received a great deal of attention in these pages, it must be recorded that it achieved a double triumph, winning both the Swedish League and Cup in handball.

Employee representatives attended a Saab-Scania Board meeting for the first time in August, while another method of disseminating information to the workforce was introduced by Scania Division, Södertälje in the form of open sessions of the works council.

Prince Bertil of Sweden has been a Saab customer since 1951. Here, Company President Curt Mileikowsky (center) and Erik Carlsson, the rally driver, deliver a Saab 99 EMS to His Royal Highness on 30 October 1974.

1974 – OLD FRIENDS

The contract for the interceptor version of the Viggen was signed with the Matériel Administration.

Old acquaintances have a habit of reappearing – and the steam engine proposed in 1972 was no exception. The idea was far too attractive – at least from the environmental aspect, which was beginning to play an increasingly important role in the debate concerning the future of the car. A new, more sophisticated design known as the ULF (the Swedish acronym for pollution-free) was developed in 1974. Basically, the system consisted of a conventional steam engine driving the wheels of the car directly and supplemented by a small ancillary steam-driven unit powering the feed water, air and fuel pumps, generator and other auxiliaries. The exhaust steam was condensed in a closed system and returned to the steam generator. However, this project was also destined to end at the development stage.

The ULF steam engine was based on the conventional steam cycle, the steam being produced in a 'generator' and expanded in a piston engine. The exhaust steam was condensed and returned to the generator in a closed system, making topping-up unnecessary. In construction, the unit was completely different from the conventional steam engine.

The hovercraft, which had failed to make an impact in its original form ten years earlier, appeared in a modified version developed in collaboration with Kockums in Malmö. The new craft was designed mainly for the Swedish Navy and Coast Guard, which had also supported the project financially. In view of the advances made in the technology during the intervening decade, this latest experimental model was expected to signify a breakthrough for the hovercraft in Sweden. However, this was to be delayed some years.

Occupational injuries caused by the jet engine fuel, MC77 (which was used both by Aerospace Division and by the RSAF), became the subject of a heated debate. The fuel was suspected of affecting the nervous system and about ten people subsequently received industrial accident compensation for injuries of this nature.

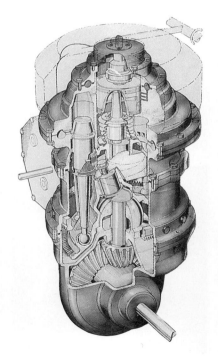

Saab-Scania acquired some of Facit's data-processing operations as a means of increasing the export potential of its products in this area. Facit was already well-established abroad, with subsidiaries in 13 and representatives in 8 countries. The acquisition expanded Saab-Scania's range of data-processing products with the addition of invoicing and electronic filing systems, as well as complete office computer systems, broadening its customer base while making the Company less dependent on orders for large, sophisticated installations.

Saab-Scania's unfinished

The Saab 114 was conceived as a turboprop-powered trainer designed to drastically reduce the cost of advanced, tactical training by replacing jets.

The Super Sonic Executive (SSE) was to be a highly exclusive corporate jet – something like a miniature Concorde.

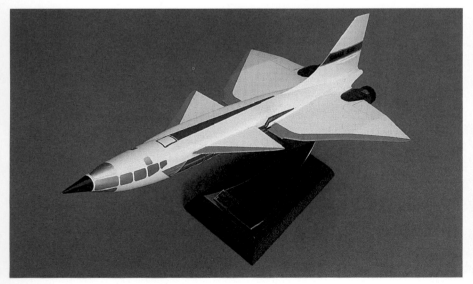

It was with a certain pride that Frid Wänström, formerly Head of Research at Saab-Scania, remarked in a 1980 interview that "Saab – as far as I am aware – is the only aircraft manufacturer in the world to have brought all its prototypes to the production stage. This is an accomplishment of which we should be extremely proud. It should and must not end with the Viggen".

On the other hand, the Company did undertake several projects which never reached the prototype stage. Whereas some were never more than a few jottings in a notebook, others progressed considerably further, one classic example being the B3LA (page 111).

One draftsman observed with some bitterness that "the closest some of the planes came to flying was when we made paper models from the useless drawings".

The urge to experiment was greatest in the case of military projects, an area in which developments moved quickly (especially during the 50s) and funds were freely available.

The Saab 1372, with a double-delta wing configuration, was an 'inherently unstable' aircraft design which took shape on the drawing board 20 years before the JAS. (In this context, the term inherently unstable means that the aircraft is not self-correcting following a maneuver, pilot intervention being required to restore equilibrium.) However, the computer technology and electronic rudder-control systems needed to fly an airplane of this type were still in the realm of science fiction, and the 1372 never became more than a dream.

The U-plane (or submarine plane) was a genuine curiosity. In this case, the 'aircraft' was to be powered by a turbo-rocket engine which, being capable of operating either as an aspirated engine or as a conventional rocket, could be based under water. With the wings folded, the plane was designed to maneuver like a submarine, before rising from the depths to attack an undoubtedly surprised enemy.

Designed as a potential successor to the Draken, the Saab 1325 was to be equipped with a rear-mounted rocket engine to boost the plane to cruising speed as required. Instead of conventional ailerons, the complete wing beyond the engine mountings was pivoted.

The problems of VTOL (Vertical Take-Off and Landing) occupied Saab engineers throughout the 50s. While take-off presented no problems (it was necessary only to open the throttle and allow the plane to lift), landing was another matter. Following a low-speed approach, it was intended to slow the plane to a 'halt' over the landing site and to descend slowly backwards to a landing. However, the 'low' speed caused the plane to ascend to 1,500 meters (4,900 ft), an altitude from which it was almost impossible to glide backwards.

Some civilian projects were also abandoned. The Saab 100 was designed as a four-seater passenger plane – which, unfortunately, did not have room for a toilet. It will never really be known whether or not the proposal to convert one of the seats into a toilet – with a screen for its enthroned occupant – was actually considered seriously! Nor is it likely to be revealed whether this or international competition put an end to the project.

The Viggen attracted international attention. One American company made inquiries for a modified version capable of flying 6 to 8 passengers at Mach 2. Unfortunately, the proposal proved to be too expensive, costing as much as a DC-9.

The 'forestry helicopter' was another unusual project. Although pine trees have roots which enable them to withstand severe storms, they are easy to uproot. The proposal was quite simply to 'park' the helicopter over the tree, attach some type of lifting device to it and pull it out of the ground – a fast and efficient method of 'felling' timber.

Although designers and dreamers alike must often have found it frustrating to see their ideas abandoned, all of the experience gained was utilized, in some way or other, in the projects which did come to fruition.

The Car Division, by contrast, does not have as many skeletons in its cupboard. The Saab 92 was a successful concept from the outset – even if most of the 15-man design team did not have driving licenses. In spite of this, they were sufficiently knowledgeable about cars to produce a basic design which remained a permanent feature of the range until the Saab 96 was finally discontinued in 1980.

In fact, the same might be said of the larger models. The Saab 99 was a basic design which provided scope for further development, as reflected in the 90. A refinement of the 99 concept, the Saab 900, in turn, provided the basis for the development of the experimental 900 Turbo 16 EV-1.

Due to lack of time and resources (not to mention necessity), no sketches of cars which failed to reach the production stage were ever made, the only exceptions being the Rally Department's experimental Formula Junior racer, the 'Monster', which was fitted with two 3-cylinder engines mounted side-by-side, and a hatchback, the Saab 98, which was based on the Saab 95/96.

Frid Wänström could have applied his comments on aircraft production equally well to Saab cars.

A full-scale mock-up of the Saab 1084. The comprehensive development work which Saab-Scania devoted to projects 1081–1084 provided a solid foundation for the rapid development of the SF340.

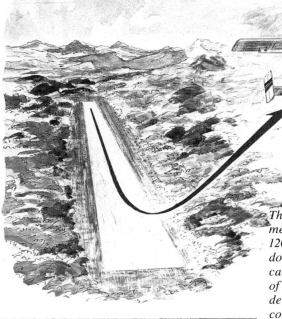

The first step towards the development of the Saab SF340 (see page 120), the 'Mule' was designed to double as an airliner and freighter, carrying 19 passengers or 2 tonnes of cargo. The aircraft was intended for service in Third World countries with poor airfields and extreme climatic conditions.

The Saab 98 was an attempt to apply the combi coupé concept to the 95/96. Although attractive, it was not considered suitable as a production model.

1975 — NEW PROPELLERS

The international recession which accompanied the oil crisis deepened in 1975. Although Sweden had possibly escaped the worst effects so far, the slump was now beginning to hurt. This was not particularly apparent in the volume of orders which, in monetary terms, remained at the same level as the preceding year and took a pronounced upswing towards the end of the year.

This was mainly due to Scania, which increased its sales to South America and the oil-producing nations. For example, exports of trucks and buses to Iraq rose by 115%. Optimism for the future was high, and a substantial investment program (which had already been approved) was implemented according to plan.

Prospects in the computer sector were not as bright. Since most of the Datasaab Division's sales were to Aerospace, the ideal solution appeared to lie in the transfer of its operations to the latter. Mainframe computers were transferred to the newly established Saab-Univac Group, while Datasaab henceforth concentrated on minicomputers.

Propellers began to turn again at Aerospace Division, although not for aircraft propulsion. Since considerable worldwide interest was now focused on alternative energy systems, Saab-Scania researchers and designers were working on the development of a wind-powered alternator, utilizing all their combined experience of aerodynamics and propeller design.

1976 — A FUTURE FOR SAAB-SCANIA?

The recession continued, creating serious problems in some quarters. The demand for many of the Company's products was unstable, while trends in both the automotive and computer sectors provided cause for anxiety.

As one means of correcting the situation, a Scandinavian sales agreement was signed with the Italian automaker, Lancia, effectively expanding the range of models to include small and medium-sized cars, while enabling the Company to concentrate its development resources on the market segment appropriate to its models.

The alarming dimensions of the problems were indicated by the remarks which prefaced the annual reviews of each of the divisions.

Scania Division reported: "The truck market worldwide is characterized by overcapacity", although 1976 was described as a satisfactory year.

The Car Division review was similarly pessimistic: "Results for 1976 have been adversely affected by the failure to offset substantial cost increases by improved productivity and higher prices".

Aircraft Division also reported problems. Despite the commencement of development studies on a new light strike aircraft and trainer (the B3LA), the report commented: "Although clarification of the B3LA situation had been expected... the Government has postponed its decision until 1977".

Another, equally interesting Annual Report was published by another Board. The company in question was Volvo, which reported a fall in profits to SKr 570 million ($114 million) and predicted further losses in the following year; resources were simply inadequate for financing and renewing its operations. In many countries, major automakers had merged as a means of overcoming such crises. Was this also the way forward for the Swedish automotive industry?

The millionth Saab rolled off the assembly line in 1976.

Sten Wennlo
Executive Vice-President, General Manager of Saab Car Division, 1976—1987

1977 – BIRDS OF A FEATHER?

What promised to be the most spectacular event of the year failed to materialize. In January, Volvo's Pehr G Gyllenhammar and Saab-Scania's Curt Mileikowsky approached Marcus Wallenberg separately to discuss the possibility of a merger between the companies.

In each case, the suggestion was prompted by the radical change in international market conditions which had characterized the industry in recent years. While European automakers were suffering from considerable overcapacity (particularly in terms of labor), manufacturers in other countries were receiving financial assistance from their governments – a factor which obviously affected the competitive situation. Furthermore, the general trend in Swedish costs was creating major problems for the export industry at a time when Japanese makers were gaining substantial ground in both Europe and the USA.

These factors apart, the merger proposal was based mainly on strategic considerations, according to the communiqué issued jointly by Volvo and Saab-Scania on 6 May.

"In an international market increasingly dominated by large groups, both Volvo and Saab-Scania are faced with a new situation. Having considered the choice between broadening the scope of existing joint ventures with foreign manufacturers and coordinating activities in Sweden, it has been decided that the latter alternative is the more advantageous. In the context of the industry internationally, both companies are relatively small. Together, however, they would make a greater impact on the world market and lay the foundation for new projects. In other words, the proposal is justified mainly by the strategic goal of creating the conditions essential to international competitiveness, thereby ensuring the viability of the Swedish automotive industry and placing employment in it on a more secure base. Under the terms of the proposed agreement, Volvo and Saab-Scania will continue, as before, to market their products in competition with each other, maintaining their existing sales organizations and marques".

Against this background and in the light of the difficulties faced by both companies in car production (both predicting losses in the sector in 1977), the two boards proposed a merger.

However, as subsequent meetings of the Board revealed, different schools of thought existed within Saab-Scania as to the merits of the proposed arrangement in both the long and short term. Skepticism increased during June, July and August, culminating in a consensus to the effect that the merger would not be in the Company's interests. In accordance with this decision, Marcus Wallenberg informed Pehr Gyllenhammar, at the end of August, that the Board of Saab-Scania was unable to recommend acceptance of the 6 May offer to its shareholders.

At this meeting, Marcus Wallenberg put his own Board's proposal that the parties should discuss cooperation in other forms. However, following a meeting of the Volvo Board, Gyllenhammar informed Wallenberg, on 28 August, that Volvo had decided to break off negotiations. In a press release issued the same day, Volvo announced that "the conditions for a merger between Volvo and Saab-Scania do not exist at the present time", adding that "it has emerged from further discussions with Saab-Scania that its management has chosen to depart from the proposal announced on 6 May". The statement continued: "Volvo can

An electric car built by Saab-Scania was tested by the Swedish Post Office for some time. The car never became a production model.

Tore Gullstrand
Executive Vice-President, General Manager of Aerospace Division, 1969–1983

The scene at a press conference held by Volvo President Pehr G Gyllenhammar, Volvo Chairman Gunnar Engellau, Dr. Marcus Wallenberg and Saab-Scania President Curt Mileikowsky to announce the plans for the merger of Volvo and Saab-Scania.

no longer await the result of Saab-Scania's internal deliberations, but must proceed with its own development program. The Company regrets that it has not been possible to reach agreement in an area of such vital importance to the Swedish transportation industry and to national economic development''.

In a press release dated 7 September, the Board of Saab-Scania announced with regret that ''it was not possible to identify areas of cooperation other than those outlined in the proposal of 6 May''. This, in effect, was the main reason for the Company's change of mind — a decision which had been reached after due consideration.

The idea of a merger had been prompted mainly by the difficulties — present and future — facing the Swedish automotive industry. Placing the industry on a viable footing would have required far-reaching rationalization measures in the areas of product development, production and sales if the potential advantages of the proposal were not to be wasted. On this basis, Saab-Scania believed that the survival of both marques following a merger would not be a realistic expectation in the long term.

Within Saab-Scania, there was a growing conviction — and an anxiety — that its cars would face a highly uncertain future in a combined company. The makes were (and are) based on different design philosophies, as typified by the use of front-wheel drive in one instance and rear-wheel drive in the other. At this time, Saab-Scania engineers had also developed the turbo concept, evidence of the advanced technology which Saab cars represented — and continue to represent.

The fact that Saab-Scania was the smaller company created a feeling of doubt that its technical concepts would find expression — an unease which was reinforced when the subject of engineering policy was raised, Volvo's attitude being that this would be a matter for the new Board.

Given the uncertainty surrounding the future of Saab cars, the Board concluded, after further intensive discussions, that the cessation of production should preferably be carried out under its own control, should the situation arise. If, on the other hand, production was to continue (as the Board fully intended), it was felt that the relevant technical and economic parameters should be determined by the Company itself. Merger was not considered to be the ideal solution to the problems.

Neither did the Board believe that truck, aircraft or computer operations would benefit generally from the merger. For example, it was considered highly probable that both Scania and Volvo would lose market shares in the truck sector. The loss of revenue resulting from any fall in sales would probably be greater than the profits accruing from joint operations. In general, the Board found it difficult to assess the exact benefits of cooperation in this area, considering the differences between Scania and Volvo in terms of product development, production and actual products.

The Board was also of the opinion that the development of both Scania and Volvo had been enhanced by mutual competition, and that each had more than held its own in the international marketplace. Competition between the two had not only been one of the motive forces for this success, but was one of the main reasons for the healthy state of the Swedish truck industry in world markets.

The Board concluded finally that the disadvantages of the merger proposal to Saab-Scania's shareholders and employees far outweighed the potential advantages. Neither did it promise that Swedish commercial life would benefit significantly in terms of greater international competitiveness.

The Board's decision to reject the proposal was to open a new chapter in Saab-Scania's history. It was time for the Company to review its operations and tackle the problems with its own resources.

The first wind generator installed at Älvkarleby – an impressive sight. Producing 150 MWh/year, the unit is 32 meters (105 ft) high and has a blade diameter of 18 m (59 ft).

With regard to the B3LA, the terms of a draft agreement submitted by the National Defense Matériel Administration (FMV) were such that Saab-Scania would be obliged to lay off personnel between 1980 and 1985, even if it received the order. In negotiating a new framework agreement, the Administration also objected to making its customary development grant to the Company.

However, a significant breakthrough was achieved in the civilian sector when McDonnell Douglas awarded the Company a contract to make wing sections for the DC-9.

Legislation to establish a major computer company by merging Stansaab and Datasaab Division was enacted by Parliament. With a workforce of 3,300, the new company (Datasaab AB) was jointly owned by Saab-Scania and the State. (Stansaab had been formed originally by these two parties, together with ITT.)

The production model of the Saab 99 Turbo was unveiled at the 1977 Frankfurt Motor Show, introducing the motoring public to a new concept – the 'Turbo'.

The Saab-Sub underwater vehicle is remote-controlled by cable. The vehicle is equipped with a film or video camera for underwater photography at depths up to 700 m (2,300 ft).

Evolution of automaking

Just as the car itself has evolved over the years, so has the technology of automaking.

The first Saabs were built almost entirely by hand – a physically laborious and demanding task (pictures 1–4).

This was followed by the development of the assembly line, each worker carrying out a specific number of operations on the car within a short period. Although the work was less strenuous, the job often became stressful and monotonous (pictures 5–7).

The assembly line was gradually subdivided (pictures 8–10), many of the simpler, routine operations eventually being carried out by robots (pictures 11–13).

The Saab 9000 is assembled using a completely new system – known as Miniline – in which the operatives work in autonomous groups, interchanging work assignments as desired (pictures 14–16).

The evolution of assembly line into Miniline is also a reflection of Saab-Scania's consistent aim of supplying its customers with cars of a more personalized character. Unless expense was no object, the assembly line provided only limited opportunities of varying the technical features, whereas the Miniline system offers wide scope for variation. Today, practically every car is built 'to order' – a trend which means that the number of identical Saabs of each successive year's model is becoming tiny.

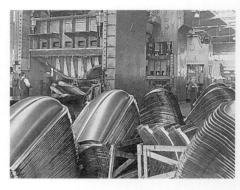

1. *As part of the Company's philosophy, the presses were used for the dual purpose of producing car and aircraft components. Since changing the dies was a time-consuming operation, large numbers of pressings were produced during each run.*

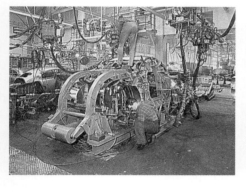

2. *The bodies were spot-welded by either the electric-arc or gas method. Since both tools and materials were scarce for several years following the Second World War, the earliest welding rods were of Saab's own design and manufacture.*

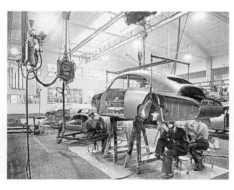

3. *The semi-finished cars were pushed from one assembly station to the next on homemade frames mounted on castors. These 'trollies' were guided by angle irons attached to the floor. Access to the underside of the body was provided quite simply by supporting it on wooden trestles.*

4. *Since building cars was a craft, daily output in the first year did not exceed three to four units.*

5. *In its time, the assembly line was the obvious method of increasing the rate of production. Bodies were transferred on skids or castors until such time as the wheels were fitted.*

6. *Once the wheels were fitted, the cars were coupled together with chains and towed to new assembly stations where the front fenders were fitted.*

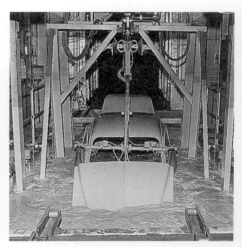

7. *One advantage of the assembly line was that certain operations which were dirty or hazardous to health could more easily be automated. Painting was one example.*

8. *The welding and grinding line at Troll-hättan prior to the 1975 annual vacation – a conventional assembly line for carrying out a series of short operations.*

9. *By the time the workers returned from vacation, the original line had been subdivided. Work on the bodies was now carried out at fixed stations, taking up to 40 minutes before all of the operations were completed.*

10. *The experiment of allowing the assembly workers to perform a series of tasks on a stationary car proved successful, and autonomous groups were gradually introduced at a number of workplaces. The picture shows the assembly of a Saab 99 Combi Coupé body.*

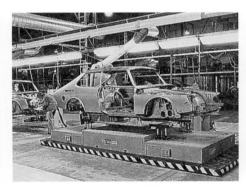

11. *Many production tools may be referred to as robots – inanimate devices which relieve humans of many tedious tasks. This carrier is used to transport cars through the plant. Remote-controlled, the device is not obliged to follow a predetermined route as were the first automated carriers.*

12. *This gigantic welding robot automatically assembles a complete body after it has been programmed for that specific car.*

13. *The system of 'one robot at each corner' is an alternative to the huge single robot. Since the devices are not restricted to one specific body, they are more flexible in operation.*

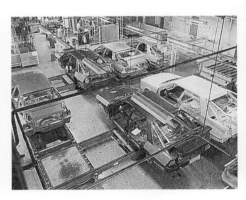

14. *One method of eliminating the assembly line, the Miniline is divided into short sections separated by buffer stores. Each section is manned by about 15 workers and the assignments are rotated.*

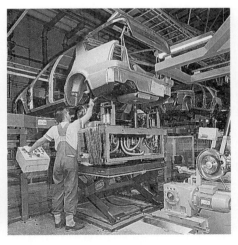

15. *Large preassembled units are fitted at each station. The picture shows a rear axle assembly being lifted into position. The body is swung outwards to facilitate access without crawling underneath.*

16. *Preassembly is important in the Miniline system. Complicated operations may be carried out in ideal working postures, while the preassembled unit can be inspected prior to final assembly.*

Saab 900

A more balanced design than the 99, the Saab 900 was introduced in 1979. The new model was 21 cm (8 in) longer and offered greater legroom. The most advanced version was a 5-door model with a turbocharged engine.

The 3-door Turbo – a sportier version of the 900.

Constant refinement of the Saab 99 following its appearance in 1967 ensured that the model never really aged, its shape being the only feature which remained more or less unchanged ten years on. By that time, however, more space was needed underneath the hood for the new turbocharged engine, while the frame also required modification for a variety of reasons, including the much stricter collision-testing standards which had been adopted in the USA.

As a result, the ongoing work on the 99 was accompanied by the design of a new model based on the 99 hatchback. However, the new version was so radically different that it was assigned a new model designation – Saab 900 – on its introduction in May 1978.

Representing a decisive step into the luxury car bracket, the Saab 900 was built initially in 3-door and 5-door versions offering various levels of performance and luxury.

Reporting on the new model, a British motoring journalist commented: ''Although the 900 is still recognizably a Saab and an obvious relation of the 99, it is somehow sexier (if a car built by those ultra-logical Swedes could ever be described as such) and is clearly in a more expensive bracket''.

Sales of the Saab 900 Convertible commenced in 1986 in the USA. This version provided ample proof that the 900 still had a great deal to offer — even after 7 years in production.

The model (particularly the Turbo) was also extremely well received in that sector of the market in which "the qualities of the car are more important than the numbers on the price tag". No less than 52,478 900s were built in the initial year of production.

The 900 series has also undergone continuous development. For example, the 1982 900 Turbo was the first model to be equipped with Automatic Performance Control (APC), a system in which engine performance is adjusted automatically to the octane rating of the fuel. This advance attracted major international attention.

Saab 900, 1978-

Length/width/height: 474/169/142 cm (187/67/56 in)
Four-cylinder, 4-cycle, 1,985-cm³, 100, 118, 145, 155 or 175-hp, longitudinally mounted engine
Four-speed manual, 5-speed manual or automatic transmission with floor-mounted gearshift
Independent suspension, coil springs front and rear
Disc brakes all round with parking brake acting on front wheels
Top speed: 160—195 km/h (99—121 mph)

1986 model
Convertible

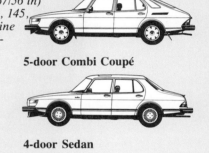

5-door Combi Coupé

4-door Sedan

The 16-valve turbocharged engine used in models such as the Saab 900 Convertible.

Exports of Saab cars are increasing steadily. The Japanese market for the 900 has grown during the 80s.

A model of the B3LA. Conceived as an extremely powerful aircraft, its armament was to consist of two Sidewinder missiles for self-defense, two RB05s and two RB11s.

Sten Gustafsson
President of Saab-Scania, 1978–1983
Chairman of Saab-Scania since 1983

Bengt Gadefelt, originator of the Saab turbo engine, was awarded the 1978 'Golden Gear' for technical innovation.

1978 — SWINGS AND ROUNDABOUTS

The controversy surrounding the projected B3LA aircraft was intense. In October, the Board received the discouraging news that the situation had "deteriorated noticeably during the summer" despite "all possible contacts with the authorities and parties involved, with the aim of bringing the matter to a positive conclusion". To put it plainly, the aircraft was too expensive and the solution simple: "We must attempt to produce a less expensive version and the industry must be prepared to take something of a gamble". A clear change in Saab-Scania policy, this was endorsed by the Board.

On the other hand, the Government expressed a willingness to assist the Company financially in establishing a more civilian-oriented pattern of operations, expressing — as on many previous occasions — its desire to maintain a somewhat scaled-down, yet adequate capacity for developing military systems. However, this transition would require time — and few believed that Saab-Scania could achieve a balance between its military and civilian operations before the end of the 80s.

A similar situation existed in the missile sector, in which a number of major projects had been abandoned and some personnel relocated. At this point, however, Saab-Scania was fully committed to the industry, and all available resources were concentrated on the RBS15 anti-shipping missile. Determined to maintain its expertise in the field, the Company joined with Bofors to establish the Saab Bofors Missile Corporation (SBMC) to coordinate future contracts.

Although the Saab Car Division reported an improvement on the previous year, the entire operation was running at a considerable loss, mainly due to the substantial resources expended on the development of the Saab 900.

Nevertheless, the development costs were small by international standards. Whereas most automakers estimate new model development costs in billions, the Saab-Scania designers had developed the 900 for SKr 150 million ($30 million) — including state-of-the-art production technology, complete with facilities such as welding robots.

Despite all, the Annual Report provided some reassurance: "This year, Scania has maintained its position as one of Europe's leading makers of heavy trucks". In terms of export sales, 1978 was yet another record year for the Division, which was now one of the world's largest exporter of vehicles over 15 tonnes. Shareholders who had read some of Saab-Scania's earlier annual reports would have been familiar with the phraseology.

On 30 June, Curt Mileikowsky resigned the post of President of Saab-Scania to be succeeded by Sten Gustafsson.

1979 — THUMBS DOWN

The B3LA project was abandoned, rejected by Parliament and Government despite the Supreme Commander's submission that it was the best choice in technical and operational terms, that it would fall within specified defense budget parameters up to 1982 (although SKr 600 million or $120 million over the conservative estimate for the period 1983—84) and that its production was essential to the survival of the Swedish aircraft industry.

Unfortunately, the Government itself appeared to have difficulty in evaluating the consequences. Saab-Scania made several requests for clarification from the

Ministry of Defense without receiving a reply, and the Government took no further action other than appointing a commission to examine the question of alternative employment should the industry be closed down.

One alternative (recognizable from another context) was the proposal that the Aircraft Division be reorganized as a separate company, with the Norwegian Government and Volvo as shareholders. In return, Sweden was to receive oil exploration rights in Norway.

Instead of the B3LA, the Defense Matériel Administration (FMV) placed an order for a new anti-shipping missile, the RBS15. As Saab-Scania's largest missile project to date, the contract (worth SKr 573 million or $115 million) was expected to provide employment for 225 people over a 5-year period.

In cars, Saab-Scania took a step towards specialization in exclusive models offering high standards of innovation, comfort and safety, top-class performance and low fuel consumption. The event was the triumphant entry of the Saab 900 Turbo into the world market.

The agreement with Lancia was expanded to include the development and production of a completely new range of cars for the 1980s. (Saab had been involved in the development of Lancia's latest model, the Lancia Delta, sold in Sweden as the Saab-Lancia 600.)

Scania's annual review featured the Division's record year in terms of sales and production, and included the information that 800 new employees had been taken on at Södertälje to keep pace with demand.

The computer sector was in a less healthy state. One report stated that "the situation at Datasaab is disastrous. The Company has not only been mismanaged, but has failed in its project to develop a new VDU and is experiencing major problems with its flight monitoring system. In addition to having made a number of ill-advised acquisitions, industrial relations are at a low ebb all round. Losses for 1979 are expected to be approximately SKr 210 million".

Marcus Wallenberg threw open his position as Chairman prior to the election of the Board. However, following appeals from both members and employees, he agreed to serve for a further year, remarking: "When one has been around for forty years, twelve months more or less makes little difference".

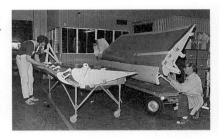

Two Saab-built wing flaps for the MD80 – the latest version of the DC-9. This continues to be one of Saab-Scania's major contract activities.

B3LA

In 1976, serious study was devoted to a project designed to develop a replacement for the AJ37 and Sk60. The new plane was to be deployed primarily as a light attack aircraft, with a secondary role as a trainer. Light, compact and inexpensive, the aircraft was to be capable of operating from a system of primitive 'bases' equipped with extremely limited maintenance sources. In terms of performance, emphasis was laid on the take-off, landing and banking capabilities, as well as on range and endurance. Capable of carrying heavy external stores, the plane was to fly at low altitude at high subsonic speeds. Furthermore, it was to be readily convertible from the training to the strike role. In the latter case, the aircraft was to be flown by a single pilot; however, the two-seater configuration was to be retained at all times.

A 1980 model Saab 99 was the last to be built at Trollhättan. Production of the model was subsequently taken over by Saab-Valmet.

Evolution of aircraft production

Most readers (at least, most of the males) have probably, at one time or another, built a model aircraft and dreamt of flying. Neither the balsa-wood parts which comprised the kits nor the method of construction differed appreciably from those used to build the first real aircraft. These consisted of frame ribs and struts, wing ribs and spars assembled to form a skeleton which was then covered in canvas. The Wright brothers' airplane, which covered a distance of 260 meters (850 ft) when it made the first manned flight in 1903, was a typical example of this construction.

Building real airplanes was also a craft requiring a high level of skill, as demonstrated by Saab's recruitment of furniture makers as its first aircraft workers. Working entirely by hand, these skilled tradesmen made not only the components, but also the dies and mould patterns. Since many of them enjoyed woodwork as a hobby, Lake Roxen (near Linköping) was home to many handcrafted timber boats, built with such feeling for the material that a visitor from Gothenburg is reputed to have said: "Those are not boats – they're floating sideboards".

It is surprising to realize that many of the 'old' methods are still used in the aircraft industry. Although tools have been improved and assembly operations simplified and rationalized (for example, by the introduction of modern lifting equipment), many of the basic principles remain the same.

Design
In the early days, aircraft were designed on the drawing board with the aid of compasses, scales and French curves. The designers drew body plans and rib profiles, calculating load-bearing areas and lifts using pen and paper. (1)

Although the design principles remain the same, the tools have been improved. In the CAD (Computer-Aided Design) system introduced in 1975, the work is carried out on a graphics monitor. Modifications can be made easily, and the geometrical information stored by the computers is used for simulation, flow calculations, and similar functions. (2)

Calculation
The foundation for the introduction of CAD technology by Saab-Scania was laid by Nils Lidbro, who developed a mathematical method of specifying aircraft shapes. The calculations were made by a team of about fifty girls trained in the method. (3)

Today, the task is carried out by computers and peripherals, the girls having been replaced by a single operator. (4)

Methods and planning

The design work is carried out in collaboration with the production planning department to rationalize the production of every component. While the design documentation is being completed, the planners prepare operation lists, assembly instructions etc. (5)

Programmable machine tools appeared in the late 60s. Today, CAM (Computer-Aided Manufacture) systems are used for programming, the geometry being transferred from the CAD data base to the machine.

The computers are used for producing operation lists, controlling material flows and so on. (6)

Machining

Many of the components are milled from large sheets of metal. In former days, this was usually carried out with a hand miller controlled by a template to produce the required shape. (7)

Modern multi-spindle milling machines are programmed with the aid of CAM systems. The numerically controlled machines are capable of producing highly intricate shapes, including components provided with cavities as an essential prerequisite to reducing aircraft weight. (8)

Materials

Materials have also developed rapidly. The earliest aircraft were built of timber covered with canvas, while the first all-metal types were built in the early 40s. The picture shows the cutting of aluminum panels. (9)

Composites began to replace some metal components in the mid-70s. A composite material consists of carbon fibers in a plastic matrix. It may be produced either as a unidirectional tape (in which all the fibres are oriented in the same direction) or as a woven fabric. The picture shows the application of preimpregnated material to a composite wing. (10)

113

Forming
Rubber pressing is an old method of sheet-metal forming which is still used today. The sheet is placed on top of a form onto which it is pressed using a rubber mat. The maximum pressure developed is 24 MPa (3,480 lbf/in²). (11)

Pressing techniques have undergone continuous development. The maximum pressure exerted by a Quintus press (which operates on more or less the same principle) is 100 MPa (14,500 lbf/in²) − roughly equivalent to the pressure exerted by 42,000 Saab 900s stacked on top of each other! (12)

Forming
Large sheet-metal components are often formed by drawing − another old method which still remains in use. The material is clamped between jaws and drawn over a die block. (13)

Composite components are formed in a completely different manner. The parts are built up layer by layer in a forming die, followed by hardening in an autoclave (see below). (14)

Assembly
In the 30s, the canvas was stitched to the timber frame and impregnated. Later, when the material was replaced by metal, the frame and skin were riveted together. However, from the early 1940s on, more and more components were assembled by bonding. (15)

Today, bonding is a common technique of which Saab-Scania is one of the leading exponents. The bonding of both metal and composite parts is carried out in an autoclave − a combined oven and pressure chamber. (16)

114

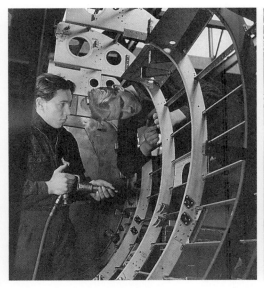

The riveting of an all-metal aircraft is no longer carried out manually. Much has been done to reduce the incidence of white fingers — the commonest occupational injury from this activity. Tools have been improved, and the level of automation is being steadily increased. **(17)**

This machine — a GEMCOR 400 — locates, drills and countersinks the holes, removes the chips, and seals and rivets the ribs of an SF340. **(18)**

Fitting
In former days, even extremely large components were lifted into position manually, causing back injuries and other occupational ailments. **(19)**

Today, practically all heavy lifts are accomplished using mechanical aids. **(20)**

Final assembly
Pictures 21 and 22 show the final assembly of a B18 and an SF340. Not surprisingly, the differences are small. The job remains a craft, demanding a high level of skill and consistently high quality standards. Modern methods of work organization give the individual technician considerable responsibility for his own work, increasing both quality awareness and motivation.

RBS15 Missile

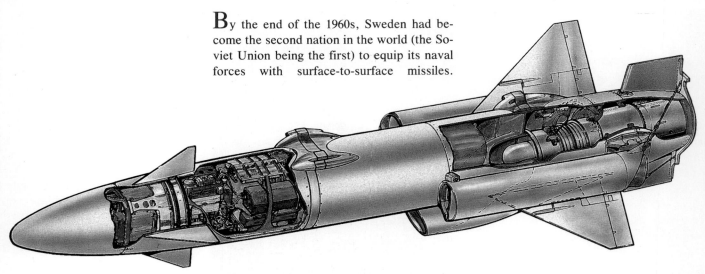

By the end of the 1960s, Sweden had become the second nation in the world (the Soviet Union being the first) to equip its naval forces with surface-to-surface missiles.

The RBS15 may also be used for coastal defense. The missile may either be fired from independent batteries or deployed as an integral part of an overall defense system.

However, the pace of development was rapid, and when the original Saab-Scania design became obsolescent, the Navy did not have the financial resources to replace it.

Not until the mid-70s did it finally seem that the fleet was to acquire a new, more effective missile possessing the particular advantage of longer range. This was to be the SKA, a combined seaborne, coastal-defense and air-to-surface weapon being developed jointly with the Air Force. However, at the eleventh hour, the Government decided to give priority to an air-to-air type, forcing the Naval C-in-C. to seek an alternative in the form of the American 'Harpoon'.

The decision was a major reverse for Saab-Scania as principals in the SKA Project. Overnight, all of the Company's specialized knowhow and experience of seaborne missile technology was rendered useless.

The situation called for urgent and immediate action. Final deliveries of the 04E anti-shipping missile designed for the strike version of the Viggen, and supplied to the Swedish Air Force during the 70s, were now in full swing. Furthermore, this weapon was adaptable to the requirements of the Swedish Navy — at reasonable cost. Apart from this, the Naval C-in-C. had already sought Government approval to install the Harpoon system on a number of vessels. Saab-Scania submitted its alternative RBS15 design in 1978 — only to find that the requirements had become stricter and that new specifications were needed.

While these events took place, amid a debate regarding the importance of maintaining and coordinating the Swedish missile industry, it also emerged that the Air Force needed an air-to-surface weapon for operations at sea. As a result, the Government decided to reconsider the Harpoon project, while Saab-Scania's engineers worked unremittingly to improve the design, in a last attempt to obtain the approval of the Navy.

In Spring 1978, Saab-Scania and Bofors AB pooled their missile technology resources to form the Saab Bofors Missile Corporation (SBMC). In April, the Swedish Defense Matériel Administration (FMV) was authorized by the Government to negotiate with the company for the delivery of a surface-to-surface missile for installation in Type T131

Norrköping torpedo boats. A second phase of the contract was to cover the supply of a similar system to the Air Force. The outcome of these discussions was the largest single contract ever awarded by the Swedish Navy and Saab-Scania's most significant missile system contract to date, the total value amounting to SKr 600 million ($100 million) in 1979 terms.

The rationale for selecting the RBS15 was based, in part, on the fact that the entire concept differed essentially from those adopted by the major powers. It was considered highly unlikely that any nation, east or west, would devote serious efforts to developing the means of jamming or neutralizing a system which was unique to Sweden.

The RBS15 was delivered officially to the Swedish Navy in Summer 1984. The entire development program had been completed in about 5 years — something of a record in the international context — and the project (employing 200 people in Sweden alone) had taken about 2 million man-hours. About a score of Swedish and foreign sub-contractors were involved.

Installed on the aft deck, the missiles are controlled by an independent firing system linked to Operations HQ. Once the targets have been ranged and the firing coordinates calculated, each missile is fired by auxiliary booster rockets, (which are then jettisoned) and powered to its target by a turbojet engine at a speed of 300 m/s (984 ft/s).

Once the homing device has been activated, the flight is completed at wavetop height, making the weapon extremely difficult to detect by radar. In the event of detection, only a minute or so is available for taking counter-action.

Weighing 780 kg (1720 lb) including boosters, the RBS15 is 4.35 m (14′3″) long and 0.5 m (1′7″) in diameter, with a span of 1.4 m (4′7″).

With a range of over 70 km (43 miles), the weapon increases the offensive range of the vessel almost fivefold.

On conclusion of the test program, the chief of the Missile Carrier Division at the Swedish Naval Establishment in Berga commented: "We've got a much better system than we ordered".

In 1986, Saab Missiles (formed in 1983) received an order from FMV to develop a mobile coastal defense version of the RBS15, confirming the 'weapons family' philosophy of the Swedish Defense Forces in a highly-important systems context.

All modern aircraft of appropriate size may be equipped with the airborne version of the RBS15.

This striking photograph shows the missile being fired from the recently commissioned coastal defense corvette 'Stockholm' at a velocity of over 1,000 km/h (620 mph).

Saab introduced APC in 1980. A refinement of the turbo concept, the system allows the engine to burn fuels of different octane ratings. In this picture, Per Gillbrand is seen demonstrating his invention.

1980 – NEW PROJECTS

As part of its efforts to become established in the civilian market, Saab-Scania undertook a joint venture with Fairchild Industries in the USA. A high demand existed for airliners carrying about 30 passengers, for use in commuter or regional traffic, offering a potential market niche to both companies. Since about 90% of the 3,500 or so commuter aircraft already in service were not equipped with pressurized cabins, they were no longer acceptable to passengers. Furthermore, the US Government was subsidizing regional carriers on a major scale. Given the encouraging prospects, the companies agreed to undertake joint development of a new commuter airliner.

In May, Parliament approved the phased replacement of the Viggen system with a new multi-role interceptor, strike and reconnaissance aircraft (known by the Swedish acronym JAS). The Bill tabled by the Government specified three main development alternatives for the JAS 'platform' – an exclusively Swedish project, joint development in partnership with another nation or straight purchase of the equipment from abroad. To examine the feasibility of the first – and obviously the most preferable – alternative, Saab-Scania, Volvo Flygmotor, SRA Communications, the Swedish National Industries Corporation (FFV) and L M Ericsson combined to form a consortium, known as the JAS Industry Group, for the purpose of specifying and tendering for a complete aircraft system of the type required.

Meanwhile, Scania introduced a completely new range of bonnet-type trucks with GVWs ranging from 16.5 to 36 tonnes. The design was based on a modular system which enabled the vehicles to be built from different combinations of components to meet individual transport requirements.

Since Scania's one major problem was a shortage of labor, management introduced the 'training' workshop – a concept which created a pool of skilled labor which was available at all times for employment where and whenever required. This was accompanied by a series of major advertising campaigns designed to attract young people into the engineering industry.

The Lancia Delta introduced the previous year was voted '1980 Car of the Year' by 52 European motoring journalists. The 4-door Saab 900 Sedan (the first version of this type) was exhibited at the Geneva Motor Show.

Datasaab had developed from being an offshoot into an operation with broadly based interests in the field of computer technology. Since the company was now outside Saab-Scania's main field of transport technology and was also ailing in several respects, it was sold to L M Ericsson for SKr 165 million ($33 million) in a move designed to enhance its prospects of development.

Dr. Björn Lundvall was elected to succeed Marcus Wallenberg as Chairman of the Board. Sadly, he had no sooner assumed the position when he was tragically killed in a road accident. He was succeeded by Gösta Nilsson, who had been president of Scania-Vabis until 1969. Marcus Wallenberg was elected Honorary Chairman.

Gösta Nilsson
Chairman of Saab-Scania, 1980–1983

1981 – EMPLOYMENT UNTIL 2000

On 4 June, the JAS Group submitted its official tender for the new aircraft. Covering the period 1982 to 2000, the total sum was approximately SKr 15 billion ($3 billion), Saab-Scania accounting for roughly 65%. The remainder of the SKr

24.9 billion ($5 billion) allocated up to the year 2000 is intended to meet the costs of armament, countermeasures, communications and reconnaissance equipment. This was the first occasion on which the Swedish aviation industry as a whole had tendered for a complete defense system. The tender sum was equivalent to an average of 8% of the estimated annual defense budget up to the turn of the century.

The commuter airliner project had already produced a design known as the Saab-Fairchild 340. Time was pressing; the first aircraft was due to be rolled out in November 1982, followed by initial deliveries in 1984.

What had once been open meadowland near Linköping was occupied, in August, by an almost complete, full-scale assembly plant covering 25,000 m² (270,000 ft²) with a further 5,000 m² (54,000 ft²) of office accommodation. Although not scheduled for completion until July 1982, the facility was sufficiently advanced to enable production of the SF340 to commence. Attracting considerable international attention, the plant was considered to be one of the best examples of a purpose-built facility in the industry.

Things were also happening at a more rarefied level. The Swedish Space Corporation approved the first Swedish-designed Viking satellite and production commenced with Saab-Scania as main contractor. A contract to produce design specifications for a communications satellite was also signed with the Corporation.

The first test firing of the RBS15 also took place with "completely successful" results.

At Trollhättan, the design engineers were forsaking the traditional drawing board in favor of computer-aided design, otherwise known as CAD. Employing computers to perform design work, CAD offers major advantages. Basically, 'drafting' is carried out directly on a VDU, all dimensions, figures and information being stored automatically by the computer. Completed drawings are then reproduced using a suitable plotter.

A unique photograph of Aerospace Division's facilities at Linköping. This is the first time Saab-Scania has received permission from the Swedish Defense Staff to publish a picture of this nature.

Saab 340

As one of the first operators, Swedair purchased ten Saab 340s for its Swedish commuter service operations. Saab expects to build and sell the Saab 340 for ten years, with the aim of supplying at least 25% of the worldwide demand (estimated at 1,500) for airliners of this type.

From the top: Test aircraft No. 2, the first Swedair airliner, the first Comair airliner, and test aircraft No. 1 (one half painted with Air Midwest's livery and the other with Crossair's) pictured on a test flight over Östergötland.

Not only one of the largest projects ever undertaken by private industry in Sweden, the Saab 340 was the first civil airliner to be built in the country since the 1950s.

Market research carried out both in Sweden and the USA had indicated a demand for a 30–35-passenger aircraft for operating feeder services to major airports. In addition, the American authorities had, at a single stroke, eased US air transport regulations, opening the way for free competition and creating a huge market for an aircraft of this type.

For several years, Saab-Scania had been working on a project known as Aircraft 108 (later renamed the Transporter), calculation and design work on the later versions of which (1083 and 1084) had advanced to the stage at which production was feasible. Without this comprehensive preliminary work, the Saab 340 could never have been designed or built in such record time.

The scope of the project was such that the initial costs and the risks involved were substantial, added to which Saab-Scania had no recent experience in marketing an airliner. As a result, the Company took another new step, seeking a partner in the venture. Its choice was Fairchild Industries, with whom negotiations were initiated in 1979.

Once in train, events moved swiftly. The Company's objective was to be first into the

Saab 340

35-seat commuter and corporate airliner

Engine type/rating	General Electric CT-5A2/2×1735 hp
Span, m (ft)	21.44 (70'4")
Length, m (ft)	19.72 (64'8½")
Take-off weight, kg (lb)	12400 (27337)
Maximum/cruising speed, km/h (mph)	507 (315)
Landing speed, km/h (mph)	154 (96)
Range, km (miles)	1500 (930)
Max. altitude, m (ft)	8500 (27890)

Derived from a military helicopter powerplant, the General Electric CT7−5A engine used in the Saab 340 is considered to be one of the most proven, economical and easily maintainable units available. Only seven simple tools are needed to dismantle and assemble the engine.

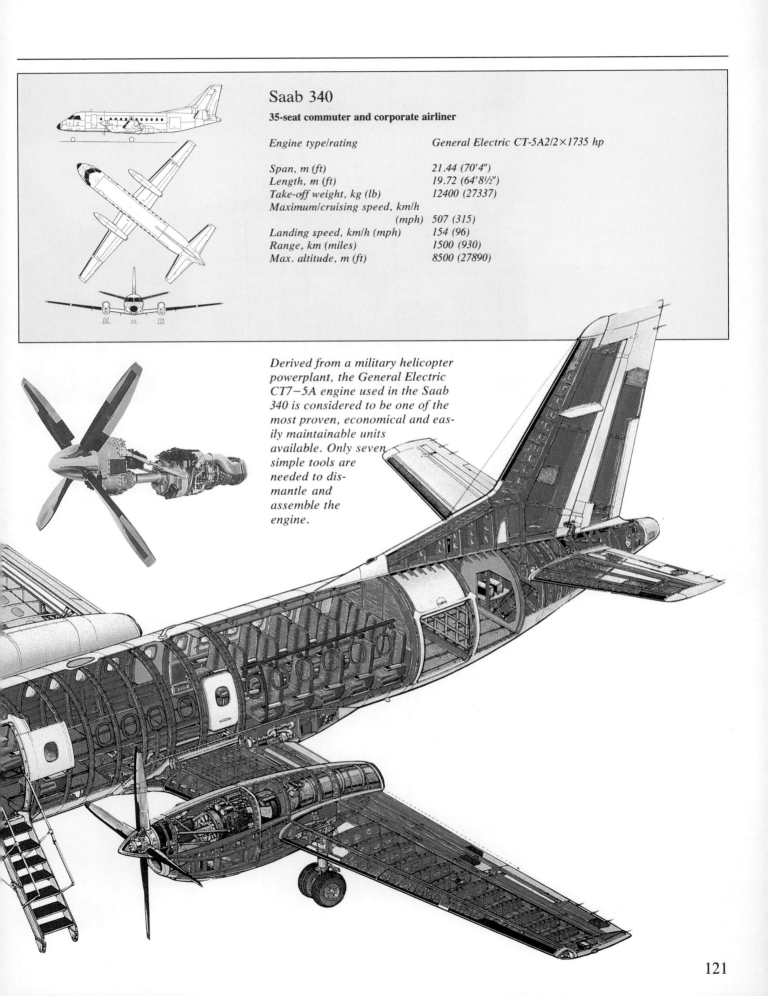

All information is displayed digitally and on CRTs. Made by Collins in the USA, the system is reminiscent of the equipment used in the Boeing 757 and 767.

American market, a feasible objective given the comprehensive development work which had already been completed and the fact that the configuration of the aircraft had been defined in less than a month. The aircraft was to be a low-wing type powered by twin turboprops, with accommodation for a maximum of 35 passengers seated three abreast. The pressurized cabin was designed to afford full standing headroom. The engine – a General Electric CT7 – was specified in June 1980, and detailed design work commenced on the following 15 September.

Meanwhile, a completely new 25,000-m² (269,000 ft²) production and assembly plant was built at Linköping – a project which was completed in less than 18 months. Under the terms of the agreement, the wings and tail section were manufactured by Fairchild and shipped to Sweden for final assembly.

More than 1,200 hours of flight testing (logged by these pilots in four aircraft) and the 'destruction' of two planes on the ground, supplemented by innumerable simulations and ground tests, were required before the Saab 340 received its certification and type approval.

The first plane was rolled out on 27 October 1982 following an impressive signing ceremony performed by King Carl Gustaf XVI, and on 25 January 1983 — three years to the day after the agreement had been signed with Fairchild—the Saab 340 made its maiden flight.

This event represented the culmination of heroic efforts on the part of all concerned, vacations having been sacrificed and overtime rules strained to the limit. Everybody was aware of the importance of gaining a foothold in the civil aviation market to ensure the survival of the Swedish aircraft industry.

The first customer was the Swiss airline, Crossair, which introduced the plane in regular traffic on 14 June 1984. The first passenger was Pope John Paul II who, as a flying enthusiast himself, declined to use the seat installed especially for him, preferring to stand in a stooping position between the two pilots, delivering a lively commentary on events during the flight and landing. The captain allowed the Pope to stand, remarking later: ''His Holiness didn't really need to sit; he was undoubtedly wearing a safety belt which was invisible to the rest of us''.

By the middle of 1986, Crossair was flying ten Saab 340s, while the Company had delivered a total of 53 aircraft to eight airlines on three continents. By this time, the aircraft had carried no less than 2 million passengers.

Faced with the need to consolidate their

financial commitments, Fairchild Industries withdrew from the project in October 1985. At this juncture, the Board of Saab-Scania decided to undertake the complete production of the aircraft, a step which required the construction of a new plant for the manufacture of wings and tail sections. With the completion of the new facility in June 1986 and the Company's takeover of the complete Saab 340 project, equilibrium was at last achieved between Saab-Scania's military and civilian production — a target which had been set at the end of the 1970s.

Several variants of the Saab 340 are available, including an executive version for 14 passengers and another for 24. Yet another configuration accomodates 15 passengers and 1,800 kg (3,970 lb) of freight.

Accommodating 34 passengers, the cabin is maintained at ground pressure up to an altitude of 3,650 m (11,975 ft).

Modern flight testing

Olle Klinker was head of the Flight Test Sector at Saab-Scania's Aerospace Division until 1986. In 1985, he became the first European to receive the Doolittle Prize, awarded by the Society of Experimental Test Pilots for his "contribution to technological advances in aeronautics".

Today's strictly scientific, high-technology test programs possess very little of the romantic 'flying helmet and goggles' aura which is normally associated with this activity. On pages 18–19, Claes Smith recounts how test flights were performed 45 years ago. Modern test programs, in contrast, involve hundreds of specialists working closely with complex computers.

The measurements to be recorded, the accuracy required, the methods to be used and the equipment to be installed in the test aircraft are all specified at the preparatory stage. During this phase, evaluation procedures must also be defined and adapted to suit the hardware and software used.

The number of readings taken in the course of a fairly routine test flight may be as high 5 million. Anything from 300 to 500 different parameters such as air speed, altitude, acceleration, flying attitude, rudder angles, pressures, temperatures are normally recorded. Many of these values are read several times per second during the flight and transmitted telemetrically to ground-based recording stations or stored by the on-board equipment.

Each test assignment is also programmed individually, depending on the aircraft characteristics and performance parameters to be tested in each particular case. For example, the different versions of the Viggen made a total of no less than 7,000 test flights. The test and flight conditions are specified individually for every flight, together with the testing and measurement procedures. Units and parameters are defined, and recording and evaluation conditions established. All of these measures are designed to assist test pilots and technicians alike to complete the program in the most efficient manner possible.

Much of today's 'flight testing' takes place on the ground. In the picture, Viggen sub-systems are seen undergoing test in a simulator of Saab-Scania design.

Despite these meticulous preparations, test programs invariably become a race against time; the delivery dates of the production aircraft are normally fixed and the time in hand is usually short. Flights must be undertaken to test an extremely large range of features under varying conditions, typical examples including different types of internal and external equipment, such as on-board navigational and radar installations, armament configurations and so on. In addition, the aircraft must be tested in a variety of attack roles and other assignments under different weather conditions.

The data and other observations recorded during the test are used to identify and correct faults, following which the complete test is repeated.

The cost of a test flight is naturally a function of the particular stage which has been reached in the program. However, the average cost of a Viggen test — which was of the order of about Skr 200,000 ($30,000) per hour of flying time — will provide an impression of the scale. The figure includes the cost of preliminary and post-flight work carried out by the test function as a whole.

Despite the use of sophisticated computer equipment, the pilot is naturally the key figure in a complex task of this nature. As already noted, every test flight may be regarded as an advanced scientific experiment in which the pilot plays the role of researcher. Without his observations and assessments, the enormous quantity of recorded information would be much less valuable. The pilot is the individual who must fly the aircraft under conditions that often impose the most extreme stresses — both physical and psychological — which the human being can tolerate. This may involve anything from prolonged spin tests to flying at low heights to test instrumentation, or flights to verify the capability of an armament system. However, flight testing is also a matter of temperament — the ability to handle an unproven aircraft

for the first time with all the attendant risks, in the knowledge that the plane may be worth anything up to Skr 100 million ($15 million).

As a result, modern test pilots are prepared for every assignment in the most minute detail. Each pilot will have spent many hours in a simulator learning to fly the plane before it ever leaves the ground. (Indeed, he may actually have been so involved in the development work that he will have 'flown' the plane even before it has left the drawing board!) The complex tasks performed by a test pilot require a thorough knowledge of aerodynamics, electronics, control systems, engine technology and instrumentation. He is the individual who will provide the engineers with confirmation that their design possesses the qualities and performance specified by the buyer.

Without the test pilot's signature on the test report, series production of the aircraft cannot commence.

Looping the loop — in which "the elevator is used to fly the aircraft through a loop, with the pilot suspended upside down at the top. If the loop is performed at an angle, the pilot will be pressed into his seat by centrifugal force" (a quotation from the Swedish Encyclopedia of 1927). This was one of the gentler maneuvers to which aircraft were subjected as part of flight testing!

The center where the 5 million or so items of information sometimes produced by a test flight are compiled and processed — a striking contrast with the early test pilot and his kneepad (see page 19)!

Cross-fertilization and innovation

For more than forty years, Saab-Scania's activities have been a unique combination of aviation and automotive technologies — which have more in common than appears at first sight.

Saab-Scania's origins as an aircraft manufacturer have had a major influence on its subsequent development, as demonstrated by the rapid advances which it has made in the fields of materials, electronics, aerodynamics and ergonomics. The Company's automaking and other operations have benefitted from the knowledge gained from research in these areas and from the practical experience accumulated over the years, both of which have been applied consistently to all its activities. In technical terms, therefore, Saab cars have proved themselves much more sophisticated than their competitors

Ejection seat
The ejection seat became an essential adjunct to the design of the J21 aircraft, in which the pusher propeller made it impossible for the pilot to bail out normally. Several alternative solutions — such as jettisoning either the propeller or the complete engine, or feathering the propeller to stop it rotating — were discussed. In the end, the designers agreed that the best solution was to eject the pilot while still in his seat — making the J21 became the first series-produced aircraft in the world to boast this feature. Shown is the testing of a rocket-assisted ejection seat on a JA37.

Aerodynamic design — a guiding principle
The lines of the first Saab car were directly attributable to the aerodynamic knowhow of the Company's engineers. Wind-tunnel tests confirmed that the shape offered the minimum possible resistance to air flow, yielding improved fuel economy.

'Aerodynamic thinking' has been used as a guiding principle in the design of both complete cars and individual features ever since then, the 'air wiper' on the Saab 95 being a typical example. Introduced in 1961, this was a method of directing the air flow down over the rear window to keep it clear of dust and dirt — an obvious contribution to greater traffic safety.

in many respects.

In recent years, many automakers have also realized the importance of access to leading-edge technology, preferably related to the aerospace industry — one reason for the recent takeovers of aircraft manufacturers by General Motors, Chrysler and Daimler-Benz.

Saab-Scania is one of the smallest automakers in the world. Its streamlined organization ensures that the links between the marketing, research and production functions are short — a feature which enables technical innovations to be translated quickly into practice. This applies both to the products and systems developed by a particular division and to those which emerge from cooperation between the different divisions of the Company.

Cross-fertilization and innovation

New wing configurations

The J29 was equipped with an engine which enabled it to approach the speed of sound. To exploit this to the full, Saab engineers began to experiment with a new configuration – the swept wing. The J29 became the world's first operational aircraft to use the new shape.

The delta wing was designed to increase speeds even further. The Draken was the first airplane in the world to boast a double-delta configuration, which boosted the speed to over Mach 2 while improving maneuverability. However, the high landing speed called for a long runway.

The canard foreplane on the Viggen – the first series-produced aircraft to use this configuration – improved the low-speed characteristics and shortened the landing run. The Gripen has a variable-pitch canard winglet which improves maneuverability even further.

'Tunnan'

Viggen

Draken

The development and manufacture of products such as satellites and ballistic control systems, and the development of missiles for military purposes, typify the application of aeronautical expertise to other areas. The sensor technology utilized in military products is also available for civilian applications, an example being the rapidly expanding field of industrial automation.

Saab-Scania's investment in research and development programs is substantial, and amounts to SKr 8.3 billion ($1.2 billion)* or 7% of total invoiced sales for the period 1981 to 1985 – a level matched by few (if any) other comparable companies.

Saab-Scania is a high-technology company numbering an unusually high proportion of highly-qualified engineers and technicians among its personnel. It has al-

Dual-circuit brake system (below)

Although two, or even three, independent hydraulic brake circuits are now accepted as standard in cars, this was not the case before 1963 – the year in which the feature was introduced in the Saab 95/96. The system was also unique in that each circuit acted on one front wheel and the diagonally-opposite rear wheel, greatly reducing the risk of skidding if one circuit was out of action.

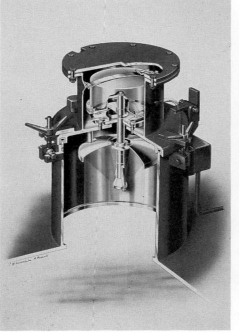

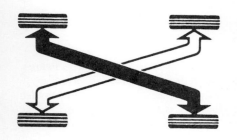

Level-measurement technology

Since the tactical value of a missile is a function of its ability to escape radar surveillance by flying at low level, its control system must be supplied with exact information regarding the height above ground or water level at every instant. Radar systems used for this purpose are accurate to within 2 mm up to heights of 25 meters.

Current energy prices make the precise measurement of liquid levels in fuel tanks essential. The flight-level control system designed by Saab-Scania for missiles has been adapted to develop an instrument for checking liquid levels in both land-based and shipboard tanks. The illustration shows, in cutaway, the radar transmitter. The antenna sends a narrow radar beam that is reflected off the surface of the liquid and back to the antenna.

* 1 billion = 1,000 million

APC — improving engine protection
APC (Automatic Performance Control) is a feature which enables the car to burn fuel of any octane number from 92 to 98. Developed by Saab-Scania, the system consists of an electronic control unit supplied with signals from three sources — the distributor, a knock sensor on the cylinder block and a pressure sensor in the induction manifold. As soon as knock is detected, the control unit commands the turbo to reduce the boost pressure, eliminating the risk of engine damage. The Saab 900 Turbo 16 was the first model to be equipped with the system.

ways been a conscious policy of the Company to promote the concept of mutual support between its various divisions and their activities — a policy typified by Saab-Scania Combitech, whose activities are described on pages 136-139. As evidence of this, the products and concepts described here include not only types developed for specific applications, but also types derived from completely different

fields — cross-fertilization in its most ideal form.

Headlamp wipers enhance traffic safety
On the basis of surveys showing that drivers seldom cleaned their headlamps until the illumination was reduced by 60%, Saab engineers in 1967 developed a system of cleaning headlamps while driving. Saab was the first automaker in the world to equip its cars with headlamp wipers and washers — an innovation considered so important in terms of traffic safety that it became legally compulsory in Sweden in 1974.

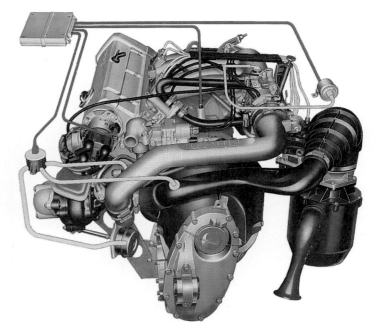

The turbo concept
Although the turbocharger was invented in 1905, Saab-Scania was the first automaker in the world to adapt it for the standard car. Scania-Vabis built the first turbocharged engine in 1951, initially for use as a power unit in rail buses. Shortly afterwards, the engines were also being used to improve the performance of trucks. Refinements in the technology led to the appearance of the first turbo-powered car — a Saab 99 — in 1977.

129

1982 — END OF AN ERA

Saab-Scania employees enjoy the use of three recreational facilities — Tunanäs, Lilla Hallmare and Örn. The picture shows the midsummer celebrations in full swing at Tunanäs.

*Harald Schröder
Executive Vice-President, General Manager of Saab Aircraft Division 1983—1987.*

It was not only Saab-Scania, but Swedish commercial life as a whole, which suffered an irreplaceable loss when Marcus Wallenberg died on 13 September. During his sixty years or so at the head of Scania-Vabis and later Saab, aviation was something of his first love. The resumption of civil aircraft production, culminating in the roll-out of the first Saab 340 on 27 October (exactly on schedule), was largely the result of his efforts. Although thirty years had passed since the Scania was built, he had succeeded in winning over all the doubters. In the words of ex-President Tryggve Holm: "He never gave up. We all had the feeling he would die with his boots on".

In the defense sphere, Parliament followed the recommendations of the Supreme Commander by granting approval for the design and construction of an initial series of 30 JAS aircraft by Saab-Scania. The decision brought to an end the often heated debate regarding the Viggen's successor.

During the year, the last activity associated with aviation came to an end at Trollhättan, with the sale of the advanced sheet-metal shop (known as the 'jet workshop') to Volvo Flygmotor.

"When car production started here, it was regarded as something of a cuckoo. And, exactly like the real fledgling, it grew so big that it pushed the others out of the nest", commented Plant Manager Rolf Sandberg at a staff farewell dinner.

Work on the Viking satellite passed a significant milestone when assembly of the complete vehicle was commenced in the 'super-clean' room at the Space Center in Linköping. (Under the terms of the contract, Saab-Scania was responsible for assembling and testing a "complete, operational satellite".) Since the Company had already built about thirty different probes and nearly twenty control systems, it was more than equal to the task.

A new, wholly-owned subsidiary, Saab-Scania Combitech, was established as

The new civil aircraft plant and offices which were built in record time to produce the Saab 340.

the optimum means of exploiting the commercial and growth potential of the high-technology spin-off products developed by the various divisions over the years. Combitech's purpose was to bring together specialist expertise in a variety of combinations, particularly in the areas of electronics, computer technology, precision engineering and optics.

Scania Division introduced two major new products — the 309-kW (420 hp) 142 H intercooler engine (the most powerful standard truck engine in Europe) and a new generation of rear-engined coaches for intercity and tourist traffic.

Georg Karnsund
President of Saab-Scania
since 1983

1983 — DUE RECOGNITION

At the Annual General Meeting, Sten Gustafsson relinquished his post as President to succeed Gösta Nilsson as Chairman of the Board. The new President was Georg Karnsund.

The maiden flight of the Saab 340 was obviously the major event of the year in the Aircraft Division. The event took place on 25 January — three years to the day after the contract between Saab-Scania and Fairchild Industries was signed.

Car Division also had reason for celebration following the visit to Trollhättan of two leading American experts on the future of the car. The visit was made as part of two extremely wide-ranging research projects entitled 'The car and its future' and 'A Japanese-American study of the automotive industry'. Summarizing their impressions, the experts commented: "You have every prospect of further success as an automaker, provided that you stick to your speciality, your unique design and your exceptional standards of quality, while continuing to improve productivity".

Eric Sjöberg and Per Pellebergs were the first test pilots to fly the Saab 340.

Gunnar Ljungström — creator of the Saab — received the supreme accolade of the engineering world when he was awarded honorary membership of the Society of Automotive Engineers. Only 142 of the world's leading engineers in the field of 'self-propelled machines' (including a bare 20 outside the USA) had ever received this distinction. In its citation, the Society noted that the award was for "outstanding leadership in the development of a small, front-wheel-drive car with superb aerodynamic qualities" and for Ljungström's "successful application of his early aeronautical experience to the car, in areas such as lightweight construction, aerodynamics, material properties and economics". The Saab-Scania design philosophy could hardly have been summarized more succinctly.

The Company was now one of the world's largest makers of turbocharged cars. Every third Saab was now a turbo, the 100,000th of which was built during the year.

The energy supply problems which assumed such major importance during the preceding decade provided Saab-Scania with fresh fields to conquer. Saab-Scania Enertech, consisting of the ASJ Group and AGA's CTC Group (following its takeover by the Company), was formed to create a competitive force in the field of energy technology. Activities were concentrated primarily on heat pumps, domestic heating equipment and district heating products.

The scene at the inaugural showing of the Saab 340 in the presence of HM King Carl Gustaf XVI. The movable partition, which kept the cold at bay when the hangar doors were open, was transformed into an impressive curtain.

Marcus Wallenberg

Dr. Marcus Wallenberg (1899– 1982) remarked on the occasion of his 80th birthday: "Anybody who has been around as long as I have, and encountered so many different people, acquires a fantastic respect for the individual. Those with development potential must be given the environment, surroundings and working conditions necessary to encourage enterprise". This was a principle which he applied consistently to his management of Saab-Scania.

Over the years, nobody contributed more to Saab-Scania's development than Dr. Marcus Wallenberg who, in 1939, played a crucial role in the amalgamation of the infant Svenska Aeroplan AB of Trollhättan and the Aircraft Division of AB Svenska Järnvägs-verkstäderna (ASJA) of Linköping (a company with which he was associated through Stockholms Enskilda Bank).

A member of the Board of Saab since 1939, Marcus Wallenberg became Chairman in 1968, holding the position until his retirement in 1980, when he was awarded the title of Honorary Chairman. His deep involvement in both Saab and Scania-Vabis provided the background to the merger between those two companies in 1969, when the company now known as Saab-Scania was born.

In a commemorative tribute written on the occasion of Marcus Wallenberg's death, Saab-Scania's President, Sten Gustafsson, wrote:

"Saab-Scania was largely Dr. Wallenberg's work. For several decades, he was a living part of the Company, giving much of his heart to its activities. Our products today symbolize qualities which he himself appreciated and could not emphasize sufficiently. His philosophy is as true today as it was fifty years ago: 'If Sweden is to become a prosperous nation, we must invest our resources in technically sophisticated products with which we can compete internationally. Furthermore, the development of high-technology industry will be indispensable to the country's independence.'

"Marcus Wallenberg often remarked: 'Let there be music' — meaning that all the many elements of a decision should form a harmonious whole, to the benefit of the nation, the Company and the individuals involved. This philosophy guided his actions on our behalf for more than five decades.

"Marcus Wallenberg was unsparing in his efforts to force through any decision which he considered necessary. When the situation demanded, he mobilized all his stubbornness and patience for the task in hand — qualities which meant a great deal to our Company. Thanks to his efforts, Saab-Scania successfully survived several crises during the interwar years, enabling Saab Cars to develop an international range of products. He also laid aside short-term interests during the late seventies when Aviation Division was going through a critical phase, lending his energetic support to the thesis that Saab-Scania should undertake the development of the JAS aircraft using its own resources and at its own risk, with the aim of preserving our technological expertise.

"Marcus Wallenberg persevered to the end, planning for the future not only with belief in the Company and its products but, above all, with faith in the people with whom he worked. His concern for all was unique, a quality which also characterized his personal relationships. On the occasion of his own 80th birthday celebrations, he remarked: 'Anybody who has been around as long as I have acquires a fantastic respect for the individual.'

"The qualities of his colleagues were always of central importance to Marcus Wallenberg. In his view, if problems existed, so did solutions — provided that the problems were thoroughly analyzed and the right people available to tackle them. In this context, he was fond of quoting his father: 'First the horse, then the cart'. In pursuit of this phi-

Saab-Scania plays host to two kings. Far left: King Gustaf Adolf VI pictured during a visit to Södertälje.

King Carl Gustaf XVI visits Saab-Scania with Marcus Wallenberg and President Sten Gustafsson as guides.

Saab-Scania was close to Marcus Wallenberg's heart, as demonstrated by his constant interest in technical developments. He is seen here with President Tryggve Holm.

losophy, he devoted considerable time to searching out the people needed for the job in hand. Possessing enormous human sensitivity and intuition, and with a huge capacity for involvement, he had a wonderful ability to fire his colleagues with the same enthusiasm.

"Marcus Wallenberg established an impressive network of contacts. His unique international connections proved invaluable to Saab-Scania, opening doors for us both onto and within the world. Aware of the importance of exports and international projects to the Company's continued prosperity, he was deeply involved in these activities to the very end."

Former Company President Tryggve Holm concluded his memorial tribute with a single brief sentence giving a succinct description of Marcus Wallenberg:

"An enthusiast of vision and energy, he possessed the will to move mountains."

Marcus Wallenberg's interest in things technical was such that he always drove the latest Saab. However, this picture shows him with President Curt Mileikowsky behind the wheel of a much older car — a 1903 Scania.

The Saab-Scania business philosophy

The business philosophy of any company must undergo constant development and change. Big or small, a company which is either unable or unwilling to adapt its thinking to keep abreast of new technological, economic and market conditions will inevitably lose the race to its competitors.

When Saab was formed by the Bofors Group, the latter's intention was to complement its aero engine production with a facility for building complete airplanes. In effect, the aim was to establish a national monopoly in the military equipment sector. However, the change of ownership which occurred only two years later changed the Company's orientation, slackening its ties with the armaments industry. Instead, the new owners successfully gathered the scattered elements of the Swedish aircraft industry into a single entity.

The demand for military aircraft naturally fell towards the end of the Second World War, posing the question of how Saab was to utilize the expertise and technical resources which had been built up. The answer was provided by the pent-up demand for cars – particularly small popular models – which was expected to be a feature of the postwar economic recovery. Dr. Marcus Wallenberg was the driving force behind the Company's decision to enter this field.

The merger of Saab and Scania-Vabis in 1969 represented a stage in the formulation of a new business philosophy in the same area. In this case, the aim was to concentrate available resources on the development of specialized transport technology. In the competitive situation which then prevailed, the new grouping had the financial strength to undertake long-term investment in major projects and to withstand fluctuations in the economic situation.

However, business philosophies – like many other economic theories – are also subject to the whims of fashion. Whereas diversification – or 'keeping your eggs in as many baskets as possible' – was the motto of the 60s, the consolidation of basic operations was considered economically safer in the recessionary 80s.

Saab-Scania has never followed the trends of fashion. Although some new activities have been created by spin-off, the Company's activities throughout the 80s have been concentrated on transportation products in a number of clearly defined market segments. These include:

1. Trucks of over 16 tonnes GVW for heavy transport applications.
2. Buses with accommodation for over 30 passengers.
3. Exclusive, high-performance up-market cars.
4. Commuter aircraft.
5. Military aircraft.

These are supplemented by products which, although not directly related to the transportation sector, are based on related technology and knowhow – activities conducted by two wholly owned subsidiaries, Saab-Scania Combitech (see page 136) which develops and builds missiles for military purposes, satellites and other high-technology products in the fields of electronics and optics (many the result of spin-off from Aerospace Division), and Saab-Scania Enertech (see page 140) which specializes in energy and flow control applications.

It may be mentioned in passing (although there are many who would prefer to forget) that Saab also attempted to establish itself in yet another area of transportation when it produced a series of small aluminum boats in the 40s.

The underlying objectives of the Saab-Scania business philosophy today may be summarized by the terms concentration, consolidation, internationalization and devolvement.

The purpose of concentration is to mobilize the combined resources of the Company in order to achieve the highest possible penetration in a highly competitive market situation.

Consolidation is aimed at creating an economic status of such strength that the Company is financially independent and is in a position to commit investment to major long-term projects. Because commitments of this type invariably entail risks, the primary objective is to ensure that the resources invested are the Company's own.

Saab-Scania invests primarily in activities related to its traditional fields of operation – product development (which it pursues consistently, even in times of economic recession), market orientation of its sales organization and products, minimization of costs by the rationalization of production methods, and improvement in the rate of capital turn-

over. Profitability targets are very well defined.

The high development costs associated with many of Saab-Scania's industrial projects frequently require the sharing of both ventures and risks with suitable partners abroad. Partners in the aviation sector include McDonnell-Douglas, British Aerospace and Boeing. The Company has also collaborated with Fiat-Lancia in developing certain components for the Saab 9000.

A natural relationship exists between the concepts of consolidation and internationalization. The viability of a joint venture is dependent on equality between the partners in terms of their level of technological advancement and the adequacy of their financial resources.

However, internationalization involves more than mere technical cooperation; it also presents an opportunity of making planned attacks on new markets. During the last decade, the proportion of Saab-Scania's export sales has risen from 44% to 64%.

Devolvement − the fourth element of the Company's business philosophy − means moving the financial responsibility for an activity closer to the market, the basic reasoning being that ancillary activities will have a greater chance of development if conducted autonomously under independent management. Enertech and Combitech are typical examples of this approach − a means of making better use of the Company's most important resource − people − and of inspiring and motivating them.

Company President Georg Karnsund has rephrased the blurb on the dust jacket of Robert Townsend's book *Up the Organization,* the original of which reads "If you are not in business for fun or profit, what the hell are you doing here?" Georg Karnsund's version is: "We are in business both for the fun and the profit". Perhaps this is the true definition of the Saab-Scania business philosophy. It is, at least, a basic concept which has been responsible for much of the Company's success.

Truck, aircraft and car − three products symbolic of the transportation technology on which Saab-Scania's operations are founded.

Saab-Scania Combitech

Saab-Scania Combitech – or COMBIned TECHnologies – was formed on 1 January 1983.

A number of Saab-Scania's hi-tech operations (many of which were the result of spin-off from the Aircraft Division) were transferred to the new company. Additional companies – particularly of the type likely to strengthen Combitech in the marketplace – were added to the Group in time.

The high – and steadily increasing – costs of research and development in all sectors of industry, particularly electronics, make it difficult for small companies to remain viable. On the other hand, large companies – despite their resources – are less flexible and major sections of the organization tend to be shielded from direct contact with the market.

Consisting of a number of small or medium-sized companies forming an industrial group under common management, Combitech's organization represents an unconventional solution to the problem. While each member company operates independently in its own market, with individual responsibility for product development, production and marketing, all cooperate in a variety of combinations to undertake joint ventures in a wide range of technologies. These may include areas as diverse as fault-tolerant computers, optics, sensors, reliability engineering, computer design, infrared technology, image processing, microwave technology, advanced control systems, microelectronics, systems technology and CAD/CAM systems.

Although this structure might – at first sight – appear to resemble a flock of sheep without a shepherd, and although time will be needed to show tangible results, Combitech's first years have been successful, indicating clearly that the concept has considerable potential.

The interactive structure of the Group and its areas of activity are illustrated by the chart below.

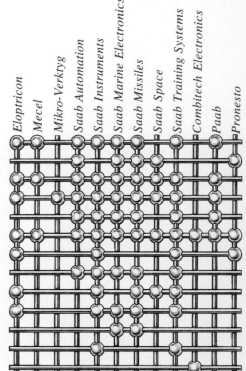

Saab Space was the main contractor for the Viking satellite project completed in 1985. The satellite is used to collect data on electrical and magnetic fields, as well as the energy content and angle of incidence of particle radiation.

The individual companies are listed horizontally, while the vertical axis indicates their respective fields of operation. As the chart shows, the concept permits the formation of large 'consortia' possessing all the resources necessary for research and development on a wide scale, while the compact size of each member company and its proximity to the market stimulates the innovative use of technology. The structure not only reduces development costs, but also shortens lead times and provides the Group as a whole with wide commercial scope.

Joint ventures may range from the exchange of entire systems to the common use of a circuit board. Notable among Combitech's products are the RBS15 anti-shipping missile (see page 116) and radar-based level measurement systems, the latter being an industrial application of a technique developed originally by Saab-Scania's missile department. This example is typical of the continuous cross-fertilization which occurs between the individual entities of the Group. Combitech companies have also developed weapons systems, passive reconnaissance equipment, military training matériel and simulators, submarine control systems and complete satellite systems.

Combitech is engaged in a wide range of

Products made by Saab Instruments include gyro-stabilized observation and sighting systems for helicopters. The picture shows the HELITOW weapon delivery system used in the Swedish Army's antitank helicopters.

activities in the field of industrial automation, with several of its companies being involved. In some cases the companies operate jointly to produce complete systems. Customers include manufacturers requiring methods of non-contact inspection and precision measurement. Several systems of this type have

Saab Marine Electronics produces a radar-based level measurement transmitter developed from a missile flight altitude controller. An example of military technology applied to a civilian problem, the device is seen measuring the ullage in a shipboard tank.

Saab-Scania Combitech

Saab Instruments has supplied control systems for the Swedish Navy's Västergötland-class submarines. Similar systems are being produced for the Norwegian Navy.

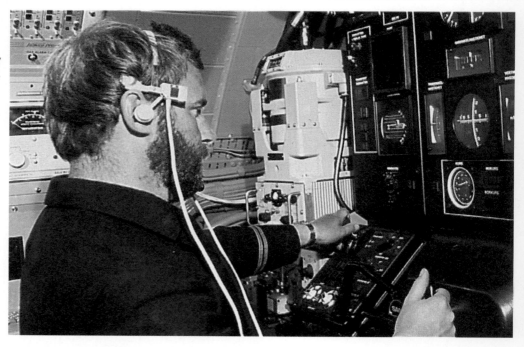

also been installed in wind tunnels and modeltesting pools. The Group's products have also been used in applications including production control, contour measurement and material flow control.

Operations such as identification, inspection, localization, measurement and control, which call for artificial intelligence are sig-

nificant areas where the Combitech companies are active.

'Horizontal' cooperation (that is, between the companies in the Group) offers the additional advantage of standardization, the aim being to concentrate on as few families of techniques as possible within each area of technology. As one means of achieving this,

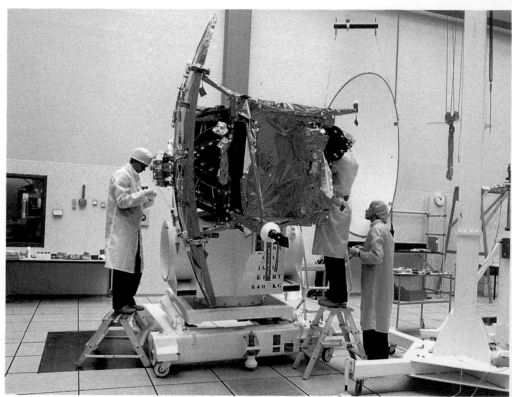

Saab Space has produced telecommunications network and command systems, computers and other equipment for several joint European satellite and rocket programs undertaken during the last 20 years. The photograph shows the assembly of the Tele-X satellite.

all design staff within the Group receive continuous information on current projects in other member companies.

No Combitech company runs the risk of being caught unawares by unexpected technical breakthroughs in its own area of specialization. All participate in monitoring international developments, while each company's lead is protected by affording it access to the activities of others in the same field. Neither does a product group necessarily incur massive costs (or, worse still, loss of customer confidence) in solving a technical problem, since the solution may already be available from another company working on advanced concepts or engaged in advanced research. In this case, the costs may be split with others interested in similar ventures. At the same time, the creativity and involvement of the smaller units vis-à-vis their specific markets are unaffected by the rules and restrictions often imposed by the demand for uniformity in larger companies.

Although Combitech does not pursue research in the true sense, it maintains close relations with institutes of technology and other research bodies. This network of contacts is expanded steadily by Combitech's employment of experts from these institutions in the in-house training programs.

During its first few years of operation, Combitech expanded rapidly in its existing fields, assisted by the acquisition of several companies and the involvement of others in the form of joint ventures. Employing approximately 2,400 people, the Group's annual turnover in 1986 was SKr 1,400 million ($200 million). Investment during the next few years will be concentrated mainly on product development and marketing. Substantial capital will also be invested in computer-based development, design, production and communications systems.

The Viking satellite was launched from the Kourou Space Center in French Guiana on 22 February 1986 aboard an Ariane rocket.

139

Saab-Scania Enertech

The Uggla brothers pictured strolling through what is now the Tannefors industrial estate. The year was 1907.

Pressure vessel testing at Norrahammar. Parca Norrahammar manufactures a complete range of heating boilers, pumps, heat exchangers, electrical equipment and hot water boilers, mainly for apartment blocks, industrial plants, public bodies and municipalities.

Founded on one of man's most basic needs – the demand for heat – Enertech symbolizes a chain of development extending from the open fire through the open hearth, wood stove, tiled stove, wood-fired boiler, oil-fired boiler and electric boiler to the heat pump.

The repercussions of the chaos created in the energy field by the 1973 oil crisis will be felt well into the next millennium. One of its effects – an explosive increase in the price of our most widely used fuel – was to make energy conservation an attractive new market.

The Saab-Scania Group had long included a number of companies involved in energy conversion and flow control. Founded in 1907 by the brothers Erland and Carl-Johan Uggla, AB Svenska Järnvägsverkstäderna (ASJ) had started to manufacture heating equipment immediately after the First World War. (Bröderna Ugglas gata, the street on which Saab-Scania's Linköping headquarters are situated, is named after the brothers.) Acquired by Saab-Scania in 1973, the compa-

CTC Osby manufactures large-size boilers for alternative fuels used in district heating plants, industrial heating and other applications. The company has gained a strong position in the market for combustion of domestic fuels.

The photograph shows a type PB 1 boiler from Osby. The painting on the boiler is the work of Linda Nyman.

ny's products were marketed under the Parca label. Parca was subsequently merged with Norrahammars Bruk (which was owned by Husqvarna), the new group being known as Parca Norrahammar AB. With origins dating from the 18th century, Norrahammars Bruk began the mass-production of castiron stoves and cookers towards the end of the 19th century.

The Group also included Svenska Armatur AB, which was founded in 1899 and merged with AB Carl Holmberg to form Nordiska Armaturfabriken in 1958. Now known as NAF AB, the company manufactures valves for district heating applications and process industry.

These companies were amalgamated on 1 January 1984 to coordinate Saab-Scania's energy technology resources. As a further measure, the Company acquired AGA's CTC Group, which manufactures a range of products covering the entire field of heating and hot-water systems.

Known as Enertech, the new Group is one of the leading companies in its field in western Europe. Employing 2,155 people, it achieved a turnover of SKr 1.3 billion ($0.2 billion) in 1986.

In terms of production, the merger created a severe problem of overcapacity, one reason being that housing construction in Sweden had fallen to one-third of its previous level. Comprehensive reorganization was not only essential, but was one of the considerations underlying the merger. The manufacture of domestic heating equipment was concentrated at Ljungby. Management-union negotiations regarding the transfer of the latter operation to Norrahammar (where a new stoving plant was being built) were opened in 1986.

Whereas Sweden provided the original companies with their traditional markets, exports now account for more than 40% of Group turnover. A further remarkable aspect is the fact that heating and heat recovery products developed after 1980 – mainly new types of oil burners, electric boilers, and alternative energy systems – account for half of sales. Energy applications contribute three-quarters of sales revenue. Domestic heating equipment comprises more than half of the products sold, installations in major apartment blocks and industrial premises accounting for the remainder.

To adapt the organization to the needs of the marketplace, Euroheat AB (manufacturing heat exchangers) was divested in 1986 to Alfa-Laval and Vårgårda Armatur AB (manufacturing sanitary fittings) to AB Gustavsberg. Following these changes, Saab-Scania Enertech consists of four business areas:

– *Heating technology:* Heating systems for single-family and two-family dwellings, special castings, enamelled vessels, heating installations for large industries and heating plants.
– *Combustion technology:* Oil and gas burners.
– *Flow control:* Gas and liquid flow control systems.
– *Service:* Energy technology advisory service, training, parts sales and monitoring of Group products.

Another member of the Group is ASJ Gjuteri, manufacturing brake blocks for railway vehicles – one of the original areas of AB Svenska Järnvägsverkstäderna.

In the light of current energy problems, heating products naturally offer a stable market with adequate development potential. However, since product development alone is not sufficient, the Enertech philosophy is to assume responsibility for monitoring the performance of its installations and training operating staff so as to ensure maximum return from the plant.

Demands on heating and energy systems will increase. To say that only one instrument – the thermometer – is used at present to control indoor climates is only a slight exaggeration. However, the systems being designed today (and the more complex types which will become common in future) also require means of controlling the air humidity, dust content and velocity, as well as noise levels and thermal radiation from various surfaces. Enertech is conducting intensive research in all of these areas.

Other areas in which new markets are opening up include energy storage and emission control. In the former case, Enertech's engineers are working on the development of different systems; these include water-based techniques and methods based on the conversion of salt from the solid to the liquid phase – a process which absorbs a high proportion of the substantial quantity of energy used, thereby, offering an excellent means of storage.

Assembly of a ballcock in a NAF-Duball ball valve. The valve is primarily intended for process control in the toughest operating conditions.

Interest in energy conservation will continue to increase, despite the major oil price fluctuations which have occurred in recent years. Enertech will keep abreast of current trends by devoting a major proportion of its resources to research into the development of more efficient and environmentally safer heating products.

Assembling oil burners at the Bentone-Electro Oil factory in Ljungby, where activities are concentrated exclusively on combustion technology.

A model of the Miniline assembly system. The system provided much wider scope for building cars to individual specifications.

This is the new Company logo which symbolizes the Saab-Scania Group as a whole. The Group's long tradition as an automaker is represented by the mythical griffin. Vabis produced its first works-built car in 1897, while the griffin made its appearance on the first Scania car in 1901. The spatial band symbolizes the Company's modern high-technology profile.

The design is by Carl Fredrik Reuterswärd, who comments: "The symbol consists of a roundel inscribed with two circles, transposed to form a cylindrical band and create an impression of optical movement. Although each is shown in its own perspective, Saab and Scania are seen as a unit".

1984 – THE BIG PUSH

For the first time, the Company produced more than 100,000 cars in a year – 102,106 to be exact. Nevertheless, it was decided to expand annual production to 150,000 by 1988. A sum of SKr 2 billion ($400,000 billion) – equivalent to 7% of total turnover – was allocated for research and development, while almost the same amount was set aside for the provision of various types of facilities. The Saab 9000 Turbo 16 also made its debut.

What was the secret of Saab-Scania's success? Outlining his manifesto in a staff magazine, Georg Karnsund, the new President, listed four contributory factors. The first was 'Technical dedication' – or the single-minded pursuit of product development, even in times of recession. Next was 'Concentration' on activities with which the Company was most familiar – transport technology in Saab-Scania's case. The third factor was 'Internationalization', defined as the drive to develop exports with the aim of increasing the current level (then running at 62% of output). (This aspect also included collaboration with foreign subcontractors.) Lastly came 'Tradition' – not in terms of conservatism or keeping to the beaten track, but of fidelity to the honored tradition of forming the technology of the future.

Aircraft construction had altered radically with the ever-increasing use of components made from composites. A subsidiary, Saab Composite AB, was formed to refine the technology, undertaking design and production assignments based on the use of such materials.

The Saab 340 (much of which is built of composites) was operated for the first time in scheduled service by Crossair of Switzerland. The plane also became the first in aviation history to be approved by civil aviation authorities in eleven countries, namely those comprising the European JAR Group and the FAA in the USA.

Scania Division introduced its new Scania 92 series of trucks – vehicles designed for applications as diverse as local distribution, local transport, construction site work and certain long-haul duties. The newly-designed engine used in the series was one of the most economical truck diesels in the world.

1985 – A NEW TECHNOLOGY

Fairchild Industries, Saab-Scania's partner in the Saab 340 project, became obliged to "consolidate its financial commitments". The original contract was revised and Saab-Scania assumed total responsibility for the project, production being transferred completely to Linköping. Like all new products, the aircraft suffered some teething problems, causing it to be grounded for a short period towards the end of the year. Although sales had been slower than expected during the previous two years, the situation now showed an improvement. This was most apparent in the US market where cooperation between regional and major international carriers was on the increase. Passengers were attracted by the plane's standard of comfort, while the airlines appreciated its low fuel consumption and simple maintenance.

The first 'flight' of the JAS 39 Gripen took place in a purpose-built systems simulator. (The Swedish for 'Griffin', the aircraft's name had been chosen in a competition.) Equipped with sophisticated aids for developing the computer programs used by the avionics, the simulator was developed and built by Aerospace Division. By this time, 2,200 people were employed on the JAS 39 project.

On completion, the Viking research satellite was handed over to the Swedish Space Corporation for launching in February 1986.

Major changes in production methods were required to attain the target output of 150,000 cars per year. Because of its low rate of output and its effects on the quality of working life, the old familiar production line had seen its day, and a new 'Miniline' system offering improved job satisfaction, greater flexibility and superior product quality was installed at Trollhättan.

The system was based on the principle of adapting the technology to the human being and making it a positive element of the job.

In the Miniline system, the assembly line is divided into small, relatively autonomous production stages in which groups of 20 to 30 operatives work within defined areas linked by buffer stations with six cars in each. This enables each group to vary its rate of output by 10−15% in relation to the scheduled rate. Individual workers are spared the monotony of a single task, while assuming responsibility for the quality of their own work. Installation of the new system was completed during the annual vacation. Technical problems associated with the initial production of the Saab 9000 caused delays, and waiting lists for new cars became long.

A new ignition system (Saab Direct Ignition, or SDI) was introduced at the Stockholm Motor Show.

As the market for Saab cars expanded, the models were to be found in countries in which owners demanded high standards of climatic comfort. The construction of a climate wind tunnel for testing a range of systems was commenced at a cost of nearly SKr 60 million ($8.5 million). In this context, it is worth recalling that the very first Saab car also underwent wind-tunnel testing.

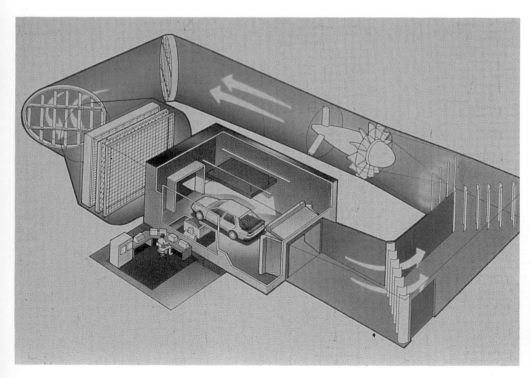

Apart from testing climate control and cooling systems, the new wind tunnel was used for performing engine starting tests, electrical system energy balances and wind noise tests.

Saab-Scania in the world market

The USA is Saab-Scania's largest market for cars. With their unique climate control system, Saabs are equally at home in Florida and Alaska.

Together with Mercedes-Benz and Volvo, Scania is one of the three leading makes of truck in western Europe — and one of the largest exporters of trucks in the world.

Saab started life as a military equipment supplier whose entire output was purchased by the Royal Swedish Air Force. Towards the end of the Second World War, however, the Company undertook a sweeping reorganization of its production resources, the establishment of a foothold in the civilian market being essential to its continued survival. In this context, cars naturally became the most important product — despite a number of internal reports which suggested the production of items as diverse as fishing reels and rowboats. (The Company did, in fact, manufacture and market a number of aluminum boats without achieving significant success.)

Although the entire output of cars was ini-

tially sold at home, it quickly became clear that exports represented the only possibility of reaching a viable production level. For obvious reasons, the first attempts to penetrate foreign markets focused on the neighboring Scandinavian countries. Unfortunately, however, all of these maintained either a total ban on imports or imposed wide-ranging import restrictions on various commodities, including cars, until well into the 50s, as a result of which only a handful of cars was sold in the first few years. To circumvent the severe duties imposed on cars imported into Denmark, several 95s were made with solid panels in place of the side windows, enabling them to be classified as vans, which were assessed at a considerably lower figure. Only after some years (following the conclusion of a three-way deal which allowed it to use Romanian credits) were the Finns in a position to purchase cars, while a few hundred cars were even sold to countries as distant as Spain and Morocco. At this time, the Americans were establishing a series of military bases in Morocco, and dollars were in plentiful supply.

Until 1956, export marketing activities concentrated more on market surveys rather than on the development of targeted sales. That year, however, the Company began to make more aggressive efforts to penetrate a bigger market, namely the USA. A number of notable rally victories achieved by the Saab 93 in that country had opened the doors, and success followed quickly. This was all the more remarkable in view of the fact that the 93 was a front-wheel-drive model powered by a 2-cycle engine — a configuration which was completely unknown in the country at that time. Since the engine burned a gasoline/oil mixture, the exhaust pipe emitted a little more smoke than Americans were accustomed to. One dealer, tired of trying to explain the phenomenon to every prospective buyer, was known to have exploded: "Okay, so this is one of the best cars in the world, but it does tend to catch fire occasionally". Efforts to develop sales were concentrated mainly on the north-eastern states (where the countryside is reminiscent of Sweden) and no less than 1,410 cars (14% of the output from the Trollhättan plant) were sold there in 1957. By 1959, nearly 12,000 cars had been shipped to the USA. Annual sales expanded gradually to about 14,000 in the early 80s, when the Turbo models and the

900 range produced a dramatic increase. In 1986, 46,000 cars were sold.

Meanwhile, sales continued to increase in Scandinavia, particularly in Finland, which became such an important market that Saab-Scania combined with Valmet to build a plant at Uusikaupunki in the early 70s to meet the local demand. After reaching a record high of 15,000 cars in 1975, sales in Finland stabilized at the present level of about 7,000 cars annually.

The most interesting European markets include Germany (particularly personnel at the NATO bases), the Netherlands, Belgium, Switzerland, Austria, France and Italy. Efforts to develop exports to Kenya, Angola, Uruguay and Peru have also been made with varying degrees of success.

Remarkably enough, a tiny foothold was also gained in the almost impenetrable Japanese market, where over 500 cars were sold in 1985 − a figure which must, however, be viewed in the context of imports totaling 50,172. Saab cars have also been introduced in Southeast Asia, the Middle East and Australia.

Originally conceived as a means of providing 'alternative employment,' the Saab car has, in time, become a product 'in its own right' and now accounts for 40% of Saab-Scania's total sales.

Saab-Scania is now one of the world's largest companies in the truck sector − an eminence achieved by a program of long-term market development and specialization in the heaviest and most exacting products in the field, specifically trucks over 16 tonnes. Following the commencement of exports in 1950, local production facilities were established in Brazil and the Netherlands in the 60s, followed by a plant in Argentina in the 70s.

Although the Middle East became a major market for trucks and buses during the 80s, the uncertainties of the political and economic situation are such that market fluctuations are severe. Heavy truck manufacture is the most international of Saab-Scania's activities, 90% of its output being sold abroad through 1,200 dealers in nearly 100 countries.

The market for military aircraft is naturally subject to completely different conditions. The B17 has been successfully sold to Ethiopia, the J29 'Flying Barrel', 105 and Draken to Austria, and the Draken to Finland and

Denmark. Countries which have purchased the Saab Supporter include Pakistan and Denmark. However, trade is subject to restrictions imposed by the Swedish Matériel Inspection Department, a limitation which has occasionally resulted in the compulsory termination of negotiations with countries considered to be at war or engaged in civil strife.

The first prohibition of this nature was imposed in 1953, when the Swedish Government blocked a major order for J29s from Egypt. Other potential contracts abandoned for the same reason have included the sale of J35s to Brazil and Argentina, and 105s to Peru, Pakistan and India.

On the other hand, the civil aviation sector is an open market in which success has been achieved in selling the Saab 340 airliner, particularly in the USA. (The Saab Safir was also a successful export during the period 1945 to 1966, when 180 airplanes were sold to foreign buyers.)

Internationalization has proceeded apace during the last decade, the proportion of foreign sales rising from 42% in 1975 to 64% in 1985. In the same period, the number of foreign employees rose from 4,700 to 8,900. By New Year 1987, Saab-Scania was engaged in operations of various types in 30 countries outside Sweden, not including the activities of independent dealers.

Since continued progress will require sophisticated products of a type which can be developed only in the context of a large-scale market, an even higher level of internationalization will be essential to the Company's future.

The Saab-Scania symbol forms a collective identification for Saab-Scania and the companies in the Group. The first pylon with the Saab-Scania symbol was erected in May 1987 at the Head Office in Linköping. The Saab-Scania pylon is now being introduced at other places all over the world.

Crossair of Switzerland was the first airline to operate the Saab 340.

From concept to reality

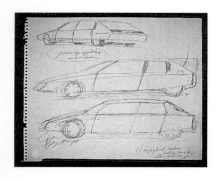

A new design often originates with a simple sketch, such as this one made by Chief Design Engineer Björn Envall (below), during a brainstorming session to discuss a new model in 1974. This was the genesis of the Saab 9000.

Whereas market research will identify the ideal type and size of a new car, engineering considerations will define the limits of the design and financial analysis will determine the permissible cost of production — added to which, national authorities will have their own views on conformity with safety standards. It might, therefore, be wondered whether the designer and his concepts actually play a major role in the development of a modern car.

The designer's feel for his task might best be summarized by the comments made by two Saab-Scania design specialists, Björn Envall and Ralf Jonsson, on the 9000.

"I must feel at home with the car — at one with it — not necessarily with every single detail, but more with the overall design. I want the car to feel comfortable and easy rather than 'big' to drive. And, although it should obviously provide a sense of power and driving pleasure, the interior should be extremely spacious.

"Smooth, gentle and timeless contours are what give the basic design esthetic value. This is the sort of shape which is most enduring — not the type which must be 'decorated' a few years later with bright moldings, skirts and so on — which is a matter of styling rather than design".

Work on a new model begins from the inside. In other words, the lines are determined only when the accommodation needs of the driver and passengers have been defined,

The first ballpoint sketch provided a basis for more specific proposals which suggested the basic design of the details.

Having decided to undertake the 9000 project, Saab-Scania threw the design open to competition between its own designers and a number of specialist firms in the industry. The winning design was this one by Italdesign.

thereby ensuring maximum use of the shape.

The designer then embarks on intensive sketchwork, ultimately arriving at a shape which also serves to demonstrate his concept to the marketing and technical specialists. Subject to their approval, a 1:4 or 1:2.5 scale model of the car is first built, followed later by a full-scale model. Built on a steel chassis, the latter is constructed from clay, using a plastic-like polystyrene foam base on which the clay is laid and worked until a perfect surface is achieved. The model is then finished with a painted foil covering. It is extremely important that the finish be as perfect as possible, since the next stage of development consists of wind-tunnel testing in which the model must resemble the actual car as closely as possible.

Testing and adjustment (as required) are followed by the construction of a new model in a rigid material, usually a plastic. An exact copy of the clay model, this is then used for making the production tools. All modifications to the basic shape (which is recorded by a computer from the outset) are entered continuously as the work progresses. Although the tools could theoretically be manufactured on the basis of the stored information, no carmaker has yet risked this step. Given that even computers are vulnerable to power fluctuations, the use of an original model to operate a copy milling machine is regarded as a safer alternative — not to mention the fact that a computer might not be fully capable of reproducing the designer's 'feel' in creating the clay model.

The creative process inevitably produces a wide range of alternatives as regards features such as the interior fittings. Although it would naturally be too expensive to incorporate all of these in models, each design is kept for further development and possible use in future models.

Design work on the Saab 9000 occupied a total of one and a half years.

Evidence that the designer does not always get his own way — the entire process being a matter of give and take between the various parties and interests involved — is provided by Ralf Jonsson's comment:

"I think the car is sensual and has attractive lines... although I would have preferred a somewhat more aggressive rear. Nevertheless, it is a shape which is capable of further refinement".

Design work on the all-Swedish interior was commencing even as the winning body was being developed from sketches supplied by the Saab Design Department. A mockup of the type pictured here is used for interior design work.

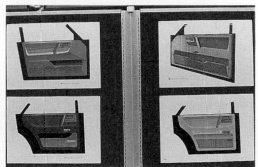

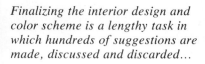

Finalizing the interior design and color scheme is a lengthy task in which hundreds of suggestions are made, discussed and discarded...

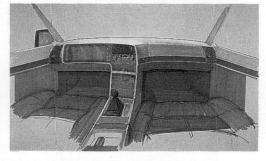

... until everything feels right. This illustration shows the basic instrument-panel layout. However, many details remain to be resolved before the panel assumes its final form.

Each individual detail receives the same careful attention, ensuring the creation of an integrated whole. The picture shows a sketch of the wheel being prepared.

Approved designs are transferred to full-scale models constructed by skilled model-builders. Only at this stage is it apparent whether concept has been transformed into reality.

147

Saab 9000

The Saab 9000 Turbo 16 was shown for the first time in May 1984 and the first buyers took delivery of their cars during Winter 1984—85. The model successfully combines the practical advantages of the station wagon with the comfort of the sedan.

In its first 20 years as an automaker, Saab produced only relatively small cars. However, the 99 — the first of the bigger models — was introduced in 1967, laying the foundation for the development of a more exclusive range with a sportier image. The trend was continued with the introduction of the 99 EMS, 99 Turbo and 900.

The effort was successful — and by 1974, the Company's thoughts had turned to the possibilities of building an even bigger and more luxurious model. However, the energy crisis called for a new design philosophy — and an answer to the question of what, in effect, was a 'bigger' car. Whereas a buyer might have defined this primarily in terms of the exterior dimensions, energy conservation factors made this criterion invalid. The problem was essentially one of designing a car which was both smaller outside and larger inside than previous models — an apparently 'impossible' feat which was nevertheless achieved. The Saab 9000 unveiled in May 1984 — although externally smaller than the 900 — was the 'biggest' car yet built by the Company.

The solution — elegant in its simplicity — was provided by combining a long wheelbase

Although shorter than the 900, the Saab 9000 has been classed as a 'large car' (the largest permissible under EPA standards) by the American authorities.

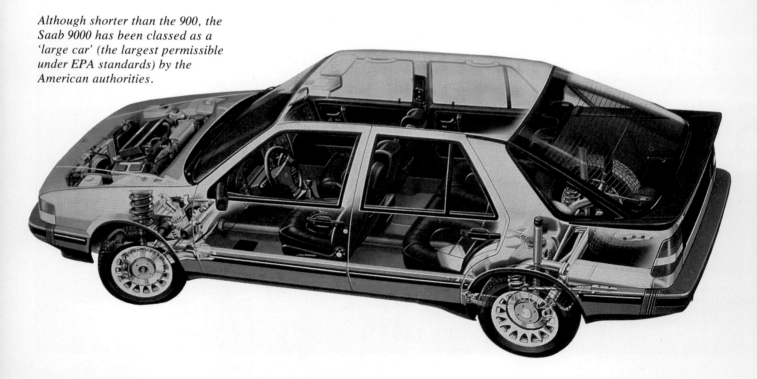

and wider track width ('a wheel at each corner') with a transversely mounted engine and the customary front-wheel drive. Overall, this combination ensured that the power unit occupied the smallest possible space, maximizing the room available for the occupants and their luggage. Unusually, the car was classed as a 'large car' under EPA (Environmental Protection Agency) standards in the USA.

The 9000 was also adjudged to be one of the most spacious cars in the world among those tested under the Swedish Autograph rules, which are recognized and applied internationally. (In this system, about 70 different dimensions are measured by laser.)

Not only spacious, the Saab 9000 is also characterized by a high standard of equipment and by impressive performance. The first version to be introduced, the Saab 9000 Turbo 16 is fitted with the most advanced version of the Saab 2-liter engine with twin overhead camshafts, sixteen valves, turbocharging and APC (Automatic Performance Control) which enables the car to run on gasoline of any octane rating. The unit is rated at 175 hp (165 hp in the catalytic converter version which uses US high-octane, unleaded fuel).

The car has a top speed of over 220 km/h (137 mph), with acceleration from 0 to 100 km/h (0 to 62 mph) in 8.3 seconds.

Saab 9000, 1985-

Length/width/height: 462/176/143 cm (182/69/56 in)
Four-cylinder, 4-cycle, 1,985-cm³, 175-hp, transversely mounted engine
Five-speed transmission with floor-mounted gearshift
Independent suspension, coil springs front and rear
Disc brakes all round with parking brake acting on rear wheels
Top speed: over 220 km/h (137 mph)

1986 model
Normally aspirated 130-hp engine (Saab 9000i)
Top speed: approx. 190 km/h (118 mph)

1988 model
9000 CD,
(sedan version)

Experience gained from ergonomic studies carried out by the Saab Aircraft Division was used in designing the driver's environment.

In 1986, the range was augmented with the 9000i 16 — a normally aspirated version possessing all the other qualities of the 9000.

The Saab 9000 underwent testing in many parts of the world, under a great variety of climatic conditions. Locations like the Australian outback and Death Valley in California subjected the climate-control system and the chassis to the most rigorous examination.

Ergonomic principles were employed in designing the driver and passenger spaces, the driver's hip joint being used as the single fixed point on which all of the dimensions were based. (Otherwise, all drivers differ in physiology.) The driver's environment was designed in consultation with Saab-Scania's aircraft designers, who are undoubtedly much more familiar with human engineering than the majority of automakers.

The chassis is designed to behave consistently under all conditions, ensuring excellent roadholding regardless of the load, the type of road surface or the speed of the car.

Standard equipment includes an interior air filter (as in the 900) which removes pollen and most other airborne contaminants. The car can, as an optional, be equipped with air conditioning and a fully automatic climate-control system which maintains the temperature at a preselected value.

Despite its spaciousness and advanced performance, the Saab 9000 is economical to run. In mixed driving (as defined by Swedish standards), the 9000i 16 returns a fuel consumption of 0.089 l/km, or 26.5 mpg (32 mpg Imp), while the Turbo 16 returns 0.092 l/km, or 25.5 mpg (31 mpg Imp) respectively — figures which have been achieved by making the car as light as possible and optimizing its aerodynamic qualities, exactly like its forerunner, the Saab 92. The link between airplanes and cars still endures!

Corrosion protection is another aspect of economy and the system developed by Saab-Scania is now (only a couple of years following its adoption in series production) one of the best in the world.

Although all new models to date had been produced by Saab's own designers, the development costs had reached such a level following the 900 that the Company decided to seek a partner for joint ventures. The choice fell on Lancia, the Italian company which was developing a similar car model and which needed to cut its costs in a similar manner.

As described by Sten Wennlo, Vice-President of Saab-Scania and head of its Car Division, 'negotiations' with Fiat/Lancia's Giovanni Agnelli proceeded more or less as follows: "The three of us — Sten Gustafsson, Wallenberg and myself — went to Geneva to meet Agnelli. After 15 minutes of discussion, everybody stood up and Agnelli said: 'Okay, Marcus, I think we'll give it a try'. 'Agreed' was Wallenberg's reply — and an absorbing five years of collaboration commenced with a handshake".

Cooperation was concentrated mainly on structural analyses and basic research into problems such as the design of support structures, the intention being that each company would retain its own identity. The value of the venture to Saab is illustrated by the comment of Giorgetto Giugiaros, Lancia's Chief

Design Engineer, on seeing the 9000: "A diamond must be judged for its beauty, not its size."

Developed in association with brake manufacturers Alfred Teves, a unique anti-lock braking system known as ABS+3 was introduced on the 1987 model.

Anti-lock brakes enable the driver to maintain control of the car even under emergency braking conditions. The system was the first of its kind to be used on high-performance, front-wheel drive cars. Unlike earlier systems, ABS+3 features duplicate safety functions based on two independent control circuits which monitor each other continuously and compare the recorded values with standard, pre-programmed settings.

A new, normally aspirated version of the 9000 was introduced in 1986. Known as the 9000i 16, the new arrival received an enthusiastic reception, one Swedish evening paper commenting: "This will be a knockout − to buyers, competitors and its big brother, the 9000 Turbo, alike". A motoring magazine wrote: "Buy two, pay for one. Here's a tip for Saab fanatics, now that more than one alternative is at last available. Any owner who places a premium on performance will obviously go for the 9000 Turbo 16. The as-

tute buyer, however, will choose the new 9000i 16 − and buy a Lancia Y10 with the change!" Might this be a novel method of extending the collaboration between Saab and Lancia?

The top-secret test program had its dramatic moments. Secrecy was so strict that becoming stranded in the 'wrong' place could create problems. Nevertheless, the true identity of the Saab 9000 was successfully concealed almost until its introduction in May 1984.

During spring 1988, Saab introduced a new model of the Saab 9000 − the Saab 9000 CD. This is a 4-door sedan with a trunk separated from the passenger compartment by a fixed rear seat and hat shelf.

Facilities at the Södertälje plant include a modern special-purpose foundry for casting engine components. With traditions dating from 1918, the foundry includes a core shop, moulding bay and fettling shop. Engine blocks and cylinder heads for Scania diesels, as well as blocks for all Saab engines, are produced here. (1)

Scania diesel engines are manufactured in Södertälje, where all types which comprise the Scania truck, bus and separate engine range are produced and assembled. The plant supplies all markets with the exception of South America. (2)

1. The foundry at Södertälje

2. Diesel engine production, Södertälje

The foundation for the Scania Division's current prosperity was laid in the 1940s. By the time peace dawned in 1945, production capacity at Scania-Vabis was five to six times what it had been at the outbreak of the war.

The strategy employed now seems self-evident; the Company concentrated on the production of heavy vehicles which (thanks to technical development and market-oriented design) were superior to their rivals and, as a result, could be sold at higher prices through a well-organized dealer network.

The destruction of most of Europe's transportation systems created an urgent demand for efficient transport media, making it vital for the Company to expand its development and production capacity on a planned basis in order to capture a greater share of this major market.

The overall level of expertise within the

3. The Södertälje transmission shop

4. Assembling gearboxes in Gothenburg

The Scania transmission plant is also located at Södertälje. Production facilities consist of three workshops. Equipped with a large number of industrial robots, the Eastern and Southern workshops are machine shops in which components such as gears and shafts for Scania transmissions, and final drives for trucks and buses, are produced. Assembly and testing of the finished units are carried out in the new transmission shop. (3)

Manual gearboxes for Saab cars are made in Gothenburg, where certain components for Scania engines and transmissions are also manufactured and finished. (4)

5. The Sibbhult foundry

6. Cab production at Oskarshamn

The Sibbhult plant comprises a foundry, a transmission shop and a machine shop. Engine blocks for Scania's V8 engine are produced in the foundry, while automatic transmissions for city buses and terrain vehicles are produced and assembled in the transmission shop. Various other components for Scania vehicles are made in the machine shop. (**5**)

Cabs are produced at Oskarshamn and are transported to the chassis shop at Södertälje. Oskarshamn also supplies CKD (Completely Knocked Down) kits to Scania's production plants abroad and to other local assembly plants around the world. (**6**)

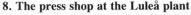

Company was raised by employing highly qualified engineers and devoting substantial resources to training and product development. The component-standardization philosophy which still forms the basis of the Division's efficient and flexible production operations was formulated at an early stage. Today, a standard, modular system is used for assembling chassis, enabling the trucks to be marketed in a wide range of purpose-built variants to suit a variety of transport applications.

At present (1986), the Division accounts for 50% of the heavy truck market in Sweden, 32% of the bus market, 12.5% of the car market (with Audi, Volkswagen and Porsche) and 30% of total vehicle registrations (excluding cars).

However, over 90% of the Division's output is sold abroad, placing Scania third

7. Production of axles at Falun

8. The press shop at the Luleå plant

Front and rear axles for Scania trucks and buses are produced in Falun. The largest industry in the area, the Falun plant has been part of the Scania Division since 1975. (**7**)

The Luleå plant is the Scania Division's main facility for the production of heavy sheet-metal pressings (side members, cross members, bumpers and final drive casings). In the latter case, the operation includes welding and machining. The finished products are consigned to Södertälje and to Zwolle in the Netherlands. (**8**)

Scania Division today

In area, the chassis assembly shop at Södertälje (where all the parts and components come together) is the largest in the plant. Built in 1968, it remains one of the world's most modern final assembly plants for heavy trucks.

In terms of production flow, the operation is carried out in three workshops – the frame shop, chassis shop and delivery/fitting-out shop. **(9)**

The entire range of Scania buses is manufactured, assembled and marketed by Scania-Bussar AB of Katrineholm. Buses occupy an honored place in the Company's history, dominating its activities during the 20s and 30s. **(10)**

9. Chassis assembly at Södertälje

10. Bus production at Katrineholm

among the world's truck exporters. The third largest truckmaker in Europe, Scania also commands 13.5% of the European truck market and occupies sixth to eighth position in the bus sector.

One-third of the Division's 21,000 employees work at the Södertälje plant, which produces more trucks than all of Scania's British competitors combined.

Parts and components are delivered to

Södertälje from the production units at Sibbhult, Oskarshamn, Gothenburg, Falun and Luleå. Each day, about 100 trucks carrying 1,000 tonnes of goods from 500 suppliers arrive at the plant. Approximately 75% of the parts used in the finished chassis are of Swedish origin. In total, Scania purchases components and materials valued at about SKr 4 billion ($0.6 billion) annually.

Scania Division today represents the prac-

11. Södertälje – the Technical Center

12. Gas engine production at Södertälje

All research and development on Scania trucks and buses and on engines and transmissions for Saab cars is carried out at the Technical Center in Södertälje. The laboratories (among the most up-to-date in the world) are supplemented by a test track which permits testing to be carried out around the clock. **(11)**

Engines for Saab cars have been developed and built at Södertälje since 1969, when the Company decided to produce its own units following the merger between Saab and Scania-Vabis. Long experience of engine design and supercharging contributed to the development of the Saab Turbo. **(12)**

156

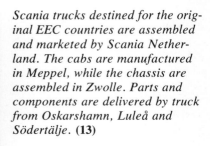

Scania trucks destined for the original EEC countries are assembled and marketed by Scania Netherland. The cabs are manufactured in Meppel, while the chassis are assembled in Zwolle. Parts and components are delivered by truck from Oskarshamn, Luleå and Södertälje. **(13)**

13. Scania's Netherlands plant

14. The Brazilian factory

Scania production operations in Brazil date from 1957. Today, the Company's plant at San Bernardo, near São Paulo, manufactures and markets trucks, bus chassis and separate diesel engines. Almost the entire output (95% by vehicle weight) is of Brazilian origin. **(14)**

tical realization of visions formulated in the 40s and 50s. However, the Company's dedicated strategy could never have become a reality without the contribution of all its employees. Without their efforts, Scania products would never have achieved the hallmark of quality for which they are now renowned throughout the world.

Scania came to Brazil in 1957, and the first Brazilian-built Scania engine was produced

in 1959, while construction of the new production plant at San Bernardo was completed in 1962. Most of the vehicles are sold in Brazil, although some are exported to other South American countries.

Production at the Tucuman plant in Argentina commenced in 1976. Apart from this facility, Scania has developed a service network covering the entire country.

15. The assembly plant in Tanzania

16. The plant in Argentina

Assembly plants for Scania trucks and buses are located in countries such as Tanzania, where CKD (Completely Knocked Down) kits have been assembled since the mid-60s. **(15)**

South America has long been one of Scania's main export markets. Construction of a second plant on the South American continent — at Tucuman in northwest Argentina — was commenced in the early 70s. Apart from trucks and buses, the plant manufactures transmissions for delivery to Brazil, in addition to certain transmission components for the Netherlands and Sweden. **(16)**

The future of motoring

A research project known as 'Prometheus' (Program for a European Traffic with Highest Efficiency and Unprecedented Safety) was launched in London in Summer 1986. Supported by most European automakers, the aim of the program is to examine ways and means of making the cars and traffic systems of the future safer and more compatible with the needs of human beings.

The traffic system envisaged is based on simple, standardized methods of communication between individual vehicles and the surrounding traffic environment — a concept which conceals the germs of a major problem, since it requires that all manufacturers agree on common standards for such communications. However, although this might appear to be an insuperable obstacle, the parties involved are optimistic. Should they fail to agree, society and the motoring public alike will provide the impetus for this type of development, based on considerations of safety and environmental protection.

In very few contexts is the interaction between man and technology more important than in the area of traffic. The millions of decisions taken as part of the interaction between drivers, their vehicles, the road and the environment, together with the inherent characteristics of this complex, exert an influence on safety and the environment alike. However, traffic capacity is also affected, as are the economies of individual drivers and the nation at large. Furthermore, the decisions involved must not only be taken rapidly, but are dependent on an infinite number of variables. The individual must collate all the information relating to the traffic situation in which he finds himself — in addition to anticipating the manner in which it is likely to change. This must then be processed to produce a decision which must be translated into action in time to avert an accident. Since this entire sequence must be performed so quickly that human senses are often inadequate to deal with it, much of the process will have to be controlled by technology.

Microelectronics have revolutionized the relationship between man and technology, one example being the development of anti-lock braking systems (ABS), the operation of which is designed to respond automatically to factors such as the speed of the car, the type of road surface and the distance to the car immediately ahead.

Around the world, major resources are being devoted to the development of intelligent systems in which computers will assist the driver to master his vehicle in various situations and traffic environments. In reality, human vision is far too limited to provide a complete picture of what is happening around the car in modern-day traffic. Relatively simple electronic aids may be used to expand the driver's field of vision, creating a safety zone (of variable size) around the entire car.

Means of communication between motorists on the road will also be improved. Automated links between the in-car computers may provide a safety network which, in time, will be developed to detect potential accident hazards and to execute the maneuvers required to avoid them. For example, this type of computerized system would give the driver sufficient advanced warning to take evasive action, overtake or brake — or, in the case of more sophisticated systems, allow the computer to take the necessary action.

A system of communications between the driver and road may be the next stage of development. A computerized system embedded in the road or laid on the surface could be used to inform the driver of his exact position, the location of the nearest free parking area, the optimum route to a specified point, the traffic density and so on.

Computerized monitoring systems will not only enhance traffic safety, but will improve traffic economics. A satisfactory system of communications between cars will eliminate many unnecessary acceleration and braking operations, while car-to-road communications will improve the utilization of road space, reducing the number of traffic jams and shortening journeys — all of which will naturally have a major influence on the overall environment.

Although technological advances of this nature might be regarded as 'pie in the sky', current developments in the fields of microelectronics, sensor design and computerization — not to mention the actual pace of development — will combine to make systems of this type available within the relatively near future.

However, all of this naturally assumes that the automakers will coordinate their research efforts and ensure that their systems are compatible. Traffic safety will certainly not be improved if one manufacturer produces 'intelligent' cars while another builds completely 'unintelligent' products. Although competition between automakers is extremely tough, all have a common responsibility in promoting traffic safety and preserving the environment – considerations which will either facilitate the sort of development outlined above or force it to come about.

In strictly engineering terms, the car of the future will be built from new materials such as plastics and composites. For example, the Saab 900 Turbo EV-1, Saab-Scania's latest experimental model, is fitted with front and rear collision shields of a composite material. Although extremely light, the components are incredibly tough, with the ability to recover their shape even after a fairly severe collision.

New materials will also be used to make cars lighter, and to reduce or even eliminate the problem of corrosion. However, such materials will also permit a considerably greater proportion of the car to be recycled. As much as 50% of the material may be recovered by melting.

The car of the future will also be designed in accordance with the philosophy already adopted in developing the Saab 9000 – a model which is built of preassembled component systems to simplify production, improve the working environment, promote more efficient quality control and facilitate servicing.

Predicting developments in cars and driving techniques within the foreseeable future is a relatively easy matter. How the driver of the future will respond is a horse of a completely different color.

The Saab EV-1 experimental car demonstrates many of the features which will typify the car of the future, including impact-absorbent zones at front and rear, solar-powered interior ventilation, high-capacity headlamps, advanced instrumentation and information systems, and invisible rear-window heating elements. The engine is an advanced Saab 16-valve, turbocharged unit developing 285 hp, giving a top speed of 270 km/h (168 mph). The EV-1 is built on a Saab 900 chassis.

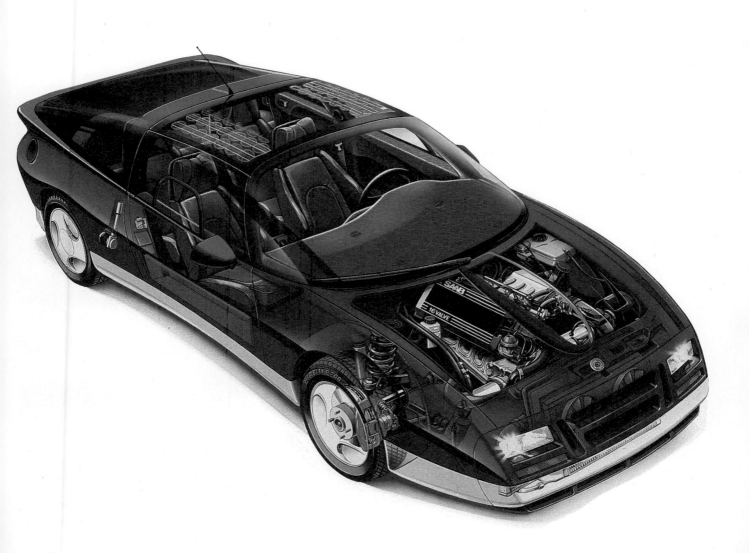

159

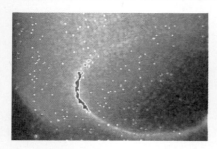

A photograph of the Northern Lights taken by the Viking satellite – confirmation of the theory that the Aurora forms a continuous ring around the North Pole.

Saab Space AB

Saab-Scania entered the field of space technology in 1967, when Aerospace Division's missile and electronics sector began work on the data and telecommunications system for the ESRO (European Space Research Organization) TD1-A astronomical research satellite, which was launched in 1972. Saab Space AB (a member of the Saab-Scania Combitech Group) was established in 1983 and now employs 200 people in space electronics. To date, the company has completed equipment contracts for 16 satellites, 18 launch vehicles, and about 30 space probes.

1986 – THE YEAR OF THE GRIFFIN

The first full-scale mock-up of the JAS 39 Gripen was unveiled on 11 February to a gathering including the Minister of Defense, the Defense Chiefs and the Press. The event signaled the completion of most of the work on the airframe, clearing the way for installation of the aircraft systems. In all, 3,300 people were employed on the project, 2,250 at Saab-Scania.

Another griffin appeared on the Saab-Scania flags raised over the old Kockums industrial complex in Malmö on 13 February, when the Company's decision to establish a new plant in the city was announced. Costing a total of SKr 3,000 million ($430 million), the projected capacity of the new facility was 60,000 cars per year, with provision for future expansion.

Scania is the Latin for the Swedish province of Skåne in whose capital, Malmö, Maskinfabriks AB Scania was founded in 1900. Like the Saab 9000, which was to be built in the new plant, the first car made by the company carried the griffin featured on the provincial coat of arms. Permission to use the griffin device was obtained from Kockums (who had also used it in their trademark), bringing the wheel full circle.

At Linköping, the new workshop built to produce wings for the Saab 340 was completed in June. Covering an area of 4,000 m² (43,000 ft²) initially, the entire complex was built in record time. Starting only after the Company had decided, in 1985, to take over complete production of the airliner, construction was completed in only five months.

The Scania Division also won two notable orders in the face of stiff international competition. The Norwegian Defense Forces placed an order for 1,700 all-wheeldrive trucks, while Bofors signed a contract for 660 off-highway trucks on behalf of the Indian Ministry of Defense.

February 22, the European Ariane launch vehicle, guided by a Saab Space on-board computer, carried the Viking satellite and a remote-analysis satellite known as SPOT (Système Probitoire d'Observation de la Terre) into orbit. With an apogee of 13,500 km (8,400 miles), the Viking's equipment included two

Two Drakens perform a low-level exercise over the old Kockums complex in Malmö, where the new Saab-Scania plant will be located.

cameras for its main assignment of studying the Northern Lights.

Series production of the Saab 900 Cabriolet commenced at the Saab-Valmet plants in Finland. The production version was displayed for the first time at the Chicago Motor Show — the largest held in the USA. Another development — the Saab 9000i with a 16-valve, fuel-injected, 2-liter engine developing 95.5 kW (130 hp) — was unveiled at Geneva.

1987 — THE SAAB-SCANIA PRIZE

Saab celebrated its 50th Jubilee. Marking the Jubilee was the inauguration of the Saab-Scania Prize for major contributions in technology. The Prize of Skr 250,000 was shared the first time. Half being awarded to Dr Günther Baumann of Robert Bosch GmbH for his work on catalytic converters and half to Bengt Gadefelt and Per Gillbrand for their development of the turbo technology.

At the Annual General Meeting, which gathered a record of over 1,500 share-holders, 15 Saab-Scania scholarships were awarded for the first time to students at technical and economic institutions in Sweden. The Annual General Meeting also established a Jubilee Fund for the employees. The Fund is planned to reach Skr 150 m.

The Scania Division completed vehicle No. 500,000 — a truck which was delivered to UNICEF. The General Manager of the Scania Division, Ingvar Eriksson, was acclaimed "Leader of the Year" by the magazine "Ledarskap" and the consultancy company "Ekonomisk företagsledning".

Saab manufactured its two millionth car. Also the last Saab 99/90 No. 614,003 — at the Nystad plant in Finland. October saw the release of the exclusive new 9000 CD model, a sedan version of the Saab 9000 to be on the market in 1988.

The Saab Aircraft Division unveiled the first prototype of the JAS 39 Gripen. The aircraft was rolled out on 26 April, fifty years to the day after the formation of Svenska Aeroplan Aktiebolaget. The Aircraft Division also delivered the first rebuilt Saab 35OE aircraft to the Austrian Air Force. Also the Saab 340B was introduced, a new version with a higher-powered engine suited for high altitude airports with high temperatures.

Car No. 2 was the fastest Saab 9000 Turbo 16 to complete the 'long run' test at Talladega Circuit, Alabama in October 1986. The car was driven non-stop for 3 weeks at 230 km/h (143 mph). Including stops for service, repairs and changes of driver, the average speed was 213.299 km/h (132,54 mph), making in the fastest-ever production model over a distance equivalent to 2 1/2 circuits of the globe.

When launched in 1986, the Viking satellite was expected to complete 1,335 orbits of the Earth. In fact, the probe's considerably longer sojourn in space will provide a unique opportunity of recording measurements over the South Pole in 1987.

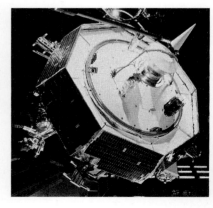

Every Gripen will be designed for deployment in an interceptor, strike or reconnaissance role. Maximum effectiveness will be achieved by equipping the aircraft for the specific mission assigned highest priority at the particular time, making the enemy's task of assessing the action capability of the Air Force much more difficult.

In the course of the sometimes heated debate on the aircraft which should be built to replace the Viggen, Conservative Member of Parliament Gunnar Björk was heard to remark: "The military want a Mercedes, but we can only afford a Beetle".

However, the Gripen will undoubtedly prove to be anything but a Beetle when it makes its maiden flight in perfect time for Saab's 50th anniversary in 1987.

This was, perhaps, predictable from the first drawings produced by the Saab engineers in October 1979. The proposal was to build a combined interceptor, strike and rec-

onnaissance aircraft, based on the loosely defined specifications of the Supreme Commander of the Armed Forces, which called for a plane half the weight of the Viggen, offering at least the same performance and costing 30–40% less. Work on Aircraft 38 (the B3LA) had been abandoned and, in the ensuing vacuum, the concept of replacing it with a multi-role aircraft proved to be in close accord with the Commander's thinking. The proposal also received the support of the National Defense Committee.

In February 1980, the Supreme Commander submitted his plans for the future de-

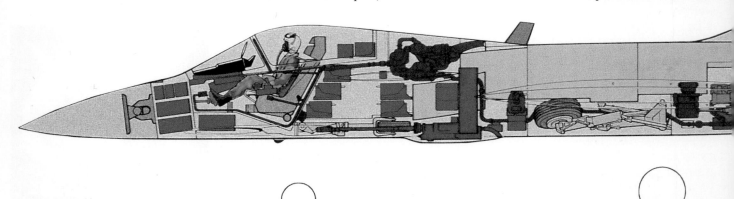

velopment of Swedish air defenses to the Cabinet. Included was a radical proposal to skip a whole generation of strike aircraft and to replace the Viggen by a new, multi-role airplane by about 1990. Only three weeks later, the Government placed the relevant Bill (incorporating most of the Commander's proposals) before Parliament.

However, the allocation for research and design work had been cut from SKr 411 million ($82 million) to SKr 200 million ($40 million), the assumption being that the industries participating in the project would contribute the shortfall. In its final report issued on 1 December 1981, the National Defense Committee noted that "the development of a Swedish aircraft may contribute to maintaining respect for Swedish security and defense policy". Parliament approved the proposal during the 1982–83 session.

Companies proposing to tender for major contracts, whether for the complete aircraft or its component systems, were required to provide substantial financial and technical guarantees. When the decision to build the plane was taken, it was predicted that the total cost between then and the year 2000 would amount to SKr 26 billion ($5.2 billion) in 1982 terms.

A consortium (IG JAS) was formed to satisfy the demands imposed on the industry by the Government. It consists of Saab-Scania

CRTs provide the pilot with flying information normally displayed on mechanical instruments in modern aircraft. The mapping display is seen in the center, with the target-ranging indicator to the right.

as systems coordinator, with responsibility for the development and production of the airframe; Volvo Flygmotor, as engine manufacturer; Ericsson, as designer of the target-ranging system, systems computer and electronic display equipment; and FFV, with responsibility for maintenance.

The designation JAS is the Swedish acronym for 'interceptor, strike and reconnais-

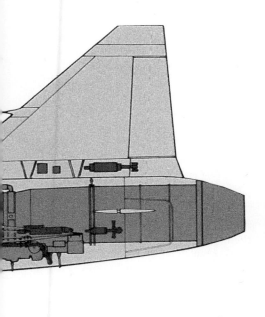

Thanks to new technologies, the Gripen is about 40% lighter than the Viggen, although possessing superior flying characteristics and performance. The picture provides a direct comparison between the sizes of the two aircraft.

The first prototype of the Gripen was shown April 26 1987, 50 years to the day after the founding of Saab.

sance'. As it indicates, the aircraft will be a multi-role type with the same pilot flying all three missions.

The plane will be equipped with advanced avionics systems incorporating radar and about 30 computers. The radar system will be the first in Europe designed for the three specified roles. The particular role will be selected by reprogramming the on-board computer system and installing the appropriate equipment — measures which will be feasible even at the most primitive highway 'bases'.

All ground service operations will be within the compass of conscript personnel.

Both this methodology and the general performance of the plane were dictated by the philosophy underlying Sweden's air defense strategy. This is based on the use of the national highway network as a system of 'bases', enabling aircraft to be stationed in a great many locations, largely immune to enemy detection.

In effect, the pilot will be a computer operator with three CRTs at his disposal — the first displaying flight data, the second plotting electronic maps of the terrain underneath (complete with details such as placenames, roads and obstacles to low-level flight) and

the third showing targets, such as enemy aircraft, identified by the radar system. Other equipment will include a line-of-sight indicator based on a holographic head-up display (HUD), featuring a bigger screen than previous types.

Commenting on the pilot's new environment, Air Force C-in-C. Sven-Olof Olson remarked: "Modern aircraft may be flown by systems — but man flies the systems".

A whole range of new technologies has been used to reduce the size of the plane (which, at approximately 8 tonnes, is roughly half the weight of the Viggen) and to adapt it generally to the demands of the warfare of the future.

The powerplant — considerably smaller and lighter than the Viggen's — uses only half the amount of fuel under equivalent operating conditions. Since the unit is also highly reliable and inexpensive to maintain, it will deliver performance comparable to that of its predecessor at considerably lower cost. The engine is a state-of-the-art American design which has been refined and modified specifically for the new aircraft.

Although the canard wing is not a new concept as such, the foreplane used on the JAS

The first airframe under construction. The new composite materials call for completely new techniques, requiring continuous on-the-job training for the assembly workers.

will be variable, acting as a control surface and giving the plane excellent maneuverability. The winglet may also be employed to provide additional braking capacity when landing, thereby reducing the required landing run. The fly-by-wire control system will eliminate all linkages between the control column and flaps, control commands being processed by computers and transmitted to the flap servos by electric cable.

Over 30% of the light alloys normally used in aircraft construction have been replaced by carbon fiber-reinforced plastics (or composites), which are 25% lighter for a given value of strength.

In principle, Parliament has approved the production of 140 JAS aircraft for delivery by the year 2000. Applying the defense price index, which allows for inflation and currency fluctuations, the original allocation of SKr 26 billion ($5.2 billion) is equivalent to approximately SKr 40 billion ($8 billion) in present (1986) monetary terms. This figure includes the aircraft, complete with countermeasures, armament and IFF equipment, as well as simulators, ground installations and other ancillaries.

To Saab-Scania, the JAS project represents a stable, long-term venture which will underpin the Company's proficiency in aviation technology. Since the military sector shows the way in many areas of development, no company which seeks to be in the forefront of technological progress can afford to confine its activities to civilian projects. Nevertheless, the project will provide an essential platform for the ongoing development of civil aircraft by the Company.

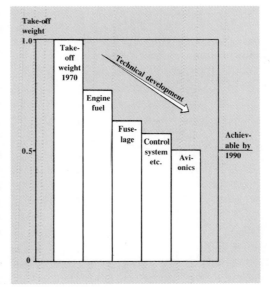

The chart illustrates the influence of technological development on aircraft take-off weights. The design performance parameters are constant.

The future of aviation

Little did aviation pioneer Otto Lilienthal suspect, as he hurtled headlong down the hills of Grosslichtenfelde in the 1890s attached to the first 'hang glider', that contemporaries of his great-grandchildren would fly to the moon.

However, he must have known that his descendants would have much greater opportunities of predicting technological developments – which in the early days of attempting to fly longer, faster and higher were limited only by technical problems.

In the field of military aeronautics, developments are dictated by completely new concepts such as strategy, logistics, altered perceptions of enemy threat and so on. Modern military aircraft are of a type which has been in existence for many years. Designed to fly at about Mach 2 at heights of up to 18,000 m (59,000 ft), they are also capable of operating at lower altitudes (although at lower speeds). These are conventional airplanes which have reached their limits in terms of performance and economy, and which will not undergo appreciable further development.

On the other hand, special aircraft of various types will obviously continue to be developed. One interesting project of this type is a high-performance turboprop designed to fly at an altitude of approximately 25,000 m (82,000 ft) and powered by solar energy, giving it almost unlimited endurance and range. This type of plane may provide a cheaper alternative to satellites, not only for military reconnaissance purposes, but also in applications such as the mapping of natural resources and meteorology.

The era of the conventional bomber may be regarded as over, certainly as far as Sweden is concerned. Although the major powers are still developing aircraft known as 'bombers', these are intended mainly for carrying nuclear weapons and cruise missiles. Within the near future, the Royal Swedish Air Force will be operating a multi-role aircraft designed for interceptor, strike and reconnaissance duties. On the other hand, the strategic scenario will be altered as countermeasures such as short-range missiles and automatic cannons are improved. Whereas air strike tactics are currently based on making a low-level approach to the target to escape radar detection, completing the mission and returning to base, future warfare will employ 'stand-off' weapons in the form of missiles designed for launching at considerably longer range, minimizing the risk of losing an expensive aircraft due to enemy action. On the other hand, new materials, combined with the extensive miniaturization of components, will greatly reduce the size of aircraft, making them much less vulnerable to enemy detection.

From now on, the heroic (sometimes almost theatrical) and gentlemanly jousts of the great flying aces will be seen only on the movie screen; the last dogfight has undoubtedly been fought. Combat aircraft of the future will be integrated more and more in total defense systems, directed from ground-based facilities such as radar stations, communications centers and command centers.

This scenario raises the possibility of aircraft becoming 'demanned', with missiles taking over. Although this discussion has raged for some time, present indications do not suggest that it will become a reality. Considerations of transport economics apart, the unsurpassed flexibility of manned aircraft presents a powerful counterargument to such a development.

One trend in the field of civil aviation suggests that smaller aircraft will be used on a much wider scale. Although this may appear paradoxical at a time when increasing numbers of people are taking to the air, it is, in fact, logical. Small airliners carrying up to one hundred passengers are easier to fill, enabling schedule frequencies to be increased while maintaining operating economy.

Major cities with large catchment areas, serving as destinations for long-haul routes, will be serviced by smaller aircraft operating regional feeder services, helping to achieve higher load factors on the longer sectors.

The feasibility of increasing flying speeds on long-haul services will also be of considerable interest. A higher speed means that the same aircraft can achieve more turnarounds, improving utilization and operating economy – the precise factors which enabled jets to make the breakthrough into commercial service. In this case, the carriers were concerned more with the efficiency of fleet operations than getting passengers more quickly to their destinations. This thinking will continue to characterize future developments.

Hypersonic airliners capable of flying at

Mach 3 or 4 at extremely high altitudes are already being discussed. For example, modern technology could be used to reduce present flight times between the USA and Japan by 80%. The level of interest among the flying public is considered sufficient to make the proposition viable. This might be regarded as a first step towards the use of trans-atmospheric aircraft, operating above the atmosphere and boosted into orbit around the earth by rockets. Although designed primarily for military purposes, such as the transport of materials to manned space stations, the possibility of flying a route such as Britain to Australia in less than two hours may create a demand for this type of airplane in the civil sector.

As in many other instances, developments in aviation tend to follow cycles. For example, the environmental pollution caused by emissions from huge aircraft, the spiraling costs of operation and the marginal savings in time achieved by most ordinary air travelers today, have resulted in the revival of one old technology in the form of the giant airships of former days. Airships capable of carrying up to 75 tonnes of bulky cargo from continent to continent at only one-fifth of the equivalent aircraft freight cost are already being built.

Although the cruising speed will be a modest 140 km/h (87 mph), the craft will basically be capable (as before) of tying up to a mast close to its destination, enabling the cargo to be delivered without requiring time-consuming transshipment or ground transport.

Although small planes will become increasingly simpler, safer, cheaper and easier to fly, they will remain the preserve of a minority of sports enthusiasts and businessmen. The enormous space which would be required to develop a functional transport system based on the widespread use of private aircraft would prohibit such a development. Existing flight corridors, in which air safety can be maintained at reasonable cost, are already filled to capacity.

It was Otto Lilienthal's dream that men should fly. To us, however, the freedom of flying as individuals wherever and whenever we might wish, must remain a dream – even for our great-grandchildren.

HOTOL is a British-built unmanned vehicle designed to carry goods into orbit around earth. With a payload of 8,000 kg (17,650 lb), it is considerably cheaper in operation than the American shuttle. The first of the vehicles is expected to be in service by the year 2000.

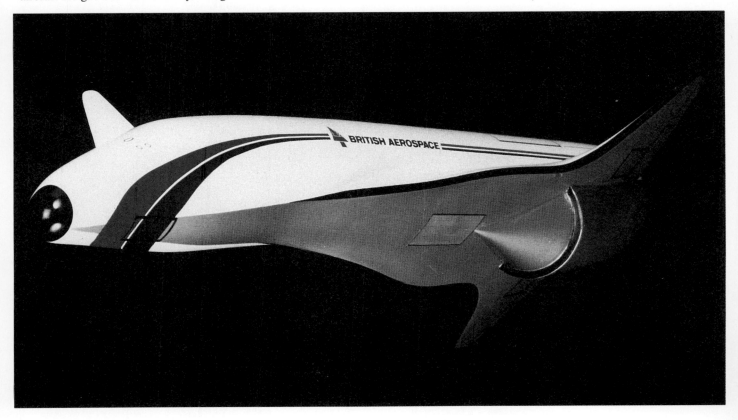

Contents

The full picture spreads in the book show:
pages 24–25: Saab 37 Viggen
pages 58–59: Series production of the Saab 35 Draken
pages 108–109: Scania 92 truck, Scania K112 bus
pages 148–149: Saab 9000

Published by
Streiffert & Co. Bokförlag HB, Box 5098, S-102 42 Stockholm, Sweden

Saab-Scania Editorial Board:
Rolf Erichs, Kai Hammerich, Gudmund Rapp,
Hans Thörnqvist and Eva Wissmark.
Other Saab-Scania contributors:
Lars Gunnar Fritz (Saab-Scania Combitech), Kurt Isgren (Scania Division)
and Peter Wide (Saab-Scania Enertech).
The contributions of a great many other individuals, both from Saab-Scania itself
and from outside the Company, are gratefully acknowledged.

Saab-Scania Editorial Committee:
Carl G. Holm, C.G. Ahremark (Saab Aircraft Division) and Anders Tunberg (Saab Car Division).

Concept and development: Streiffert & Co., in consultation with Saab-Scania.
Research and text: Björn Olson, Aktiv Bild, Gothenburg.
Layout: Paul Eklund and Nils Hermanson.
Technical production: Johnston & Co., Gothenburg.
Cover: Edition Franco Maria Ricci, Milan.
Cover photographs: Hans Hammarskiöld.
Typesetting, reproduction and printing: Ljungföretagen, Örebro 1987.
English translation by Tom Byrne, Techtrans Ireland, Cork
Editing (English edition): Johnston & Co., Gothenburg

Photographs: Endpapers: Hans Hammarskiöld; p 6: Enoch Thulin — Pressens Bild; pp 18—19: Lennart Nilsson; p 51: Bo Dahlin; p 66: Peter Haventon; p 70: DC3 — Ola Nilsson/Svenskt Pressfoto; p 71: Concorde — Keystone/Svenskt Pressfoto; p 108: Hans Hammarskiöld; p 139: Arianespace; pp 154—157: Bo Malmgren and Carl Erik Andersson; p 160: Kockums — Urban Mörén; p 163: Gripens instrument panel — Ericsson AB; p 165: testing the Gripen engine—Volvo Flygmotor; p 167: British Aerospace. Other pictures by Saab-Scania staff photographers and from Company archives.

ISBN 91-7886-024-5